D1493185

THE DAY SHAKESPEARE DIED

THE DAY
SHAKESPEARE DIED

Hugh Ross Williamson

London
MICHAEL JOSEPH

First published by
MICHAEL JOSEPH LTD
26 Bloomsbury Street
*London, W.C.*1
1962

© *copyright 1962 by Hugh Ross Williamson*

Set and printed in Great Britain by Tonbridge Printers Ltd,
Peach Hall Works, Tonbridge, Kent, in Baskerville eleven
on thirteen point, on paper made by Henry Bruce at Currie,
Midlothian, and bound by James Burn at Esher, Surrey

To

BASIL SCOTT WHITE

with affection and gratitude

Contents

Preface

AN alternative title for this little book might be 'Shakespeare in Context and Perspective,' but such a phrase might deceive the reader into imagining that it was an academic tome, whereas its writing is the outcome of a lifetime's mounting irritation with academic tomes which have nothing to do with Shakespeare but only with the Shakespeare Industry.

In viewing any man's life there are, it seems to me, three aspects to consider—his relation to God, his work, and his place in the society of his time. It is into these three sections, loosely, that this essay falls; and if the first may seem disproportionately long, it is only because it is the most important and the most difficult to establish in face of the false assumptions which underlie conventional teaching about sixteenth and seventeenth century England.

Personally I agree with the verdict that 'the greatest thing the English have done in the world yet is to produce Shakespeare.' Yet many who would not dissent from this find themselves unwilling to face the actual object of this greatness – a Catholic actor-playwright who was of no particular account to his contemporaries. By trying to put him in his true context, I hope I may have a little restored perspective.

HUGH ROSS WILLIAMSON

London
Ss. Cyril and Methodius, 1961

I : The Question

ON St George's Day, 1616, the day on which he entered his fifty-third year, William Shakespeare died at New Place, his mansion at Stratford-on-Avon. For so public a figure, his death, like so much of his life, has a strange anonymity and he managed to elude posterity even in his passing. For two days, it is said, his body lay in state in his grand house; but there remains no account of the funeral. His tomb is in the chancel of Stratford Church, though it is possible that his body does not lie in it. At least he made sure that no one would be temerarious enough to look. The doggerel verse he ordered to be put on his nameless grave:

> Good Friend, for Jesus's sake forbear
> To dig the dust enclosed here!
> Blest be the man that spares these stones
> And curst be he that moves my bones

made it impossible even for his widow, dying seven years later, to lie with him in death. And the tradition that his grave was dug seventeen feet deep (a major improbability so near the river) only serves to underline the ambiguity.

The Reverend Richard Davies, a Gloucestershire clergyman, noted, about seventy years after Shakespeare's death, that the inscription had laid 'a heavy curse upon anyone who shall remove his bones' and added: 'He died a Papist.' There is no ground for supposing this information inaccurate, especially as William Shakespeare's father and mother were both open and practising Catholics all their lives. Sir Sidney

Lee's contradictory remark that Shakespeare 'was to the last a conforming member of the Church of England' has, like so much of Lee's work on Shakespeare, been discredited by Sir Edmund Chambers' monumental volumes; and had Sidney Lee not abandoned his real name, Solomon Lazarus,* he might have been less uncritically accepted in the first place as an authority on Anglicanism.

The crucial point about the day Shakespeare died is not what faith he died in or where he was actually buried, but whether or not he was able to have the ministrations of a Catholic priest at his death-bed and whether he was given a Catholic burial.

The question of Shakespeare's religion also affects the years of his retirement at Stratford, about which such conflicting speculations have been made. The Victorians, Edwardians and many of the Georgians, since they had neither the experience to understand nor the learning to appreciate the realities of the Jacobean scene, tended to think of it, albeit unconsciously, in terms of Alfred Lord Tennyson in the Isle of Wight, whereas it was more like one of the literary figures of a Resistance Movement in occupied territory.

The tributes today read a trifle oddly. There is Furnivall's 'forgiving and forgiven, full of the highest wisdom and peace, at one with family and friends and foes, in harmony with Avon's flow and Stratford's level meads, Shakespeare closed his life on earth.' There is Dowden's comparison of him to a ship 'entering harbour with sails full set to anchor in peace.' There is Chambers' picture of 'the open fields and cool water-meadows and woodland of Stratford' among which 'he lived upon friendly terms, not only with the leading citizens, but with the well-to-do gentry of the town and its neighbourhood.'

Contradicting these is Lytton Strachey's famous essay, written in 1906, which imagines him 'bored with people,

* See the article on him in the Dictionary of National Biography.

bored with real life, bored with drama, bored, in fact, with everything except poetry and poetical dreams.' Strachey however – and it was the real point of his attack on the sentimentalists – had at least realised the depth of Shakespeare's despair. 'Bottom was the first of Shakespeare's masterpieces in characterisation, Caliban was the last; and what a world of bitterness and horror lies between them!' If he did not understand the cause of it, his perception of the fact brought a breath of reality into the argument. But almost immediately the new insight was romanticised. Frank Harris, in 1909, improving on Strachey, provided (without an iota of either evidence or probability) the reason for Shakespeare's despair: 'The passions of lust and jealousy and rage had at length worn out Shakespeare's strength and, after trying in vain to win serenity in *The Tempest*, he crept home to Stratford to die. In his native air, I imagine, his health gradually improved; but he was never strong enough to venture back to residence in London.'

Other critics, as Professor Tillyard has noticed, see Shakespeare, having recovered from 'the Dark Lady' 'doting with benevolent purity on his now mature young daughter, under the successive forms of Marina, Imogen, Perdita and Miranda.' As Judith Shakespeare was in her late twenties when Shakespeare retired to Stratford (Miranda, it will be remembered, was fourteen) this speculation is hardly convincing. At the age of thirty-one, Judith managed to procure one of her childhood friends as a husband and married him ten weeks before her father's death (for some reason the couple were excommunicated) and her elder sister, Susanna, the wife of the local physician, was, two years after Shakespeare's retirement, the subject of a slander action, in which her husband sued a young Stratfordian for a remark which not only reflected on her morals but specified the person and the place. It seems unlikely that Shakespeare's view of either daughter can be correctly described as 'doting with benevolent purity.'

What is more to the point in the last plays is that they are indisputably Christian. Conflicting theories to explain the change in their outlook are among the commonplaces of modern criticism. Sir Edmund Chambers suggests a nervous breakdown, followed by a kind of 'conversion' – which would not be incompatible with the interpretation (which seems to me more probable) that Shakespeare after the death of his uncompromisingly Catholic mother in 1608 decided no longer to conceal his faith. One is almost tempted to read an intentional ambiguity into Coriolanus's words to Volumnia, written in that year:

> O mother, mother!
> What have you done? Behold the heavens do ope,
> The gods look down, and this unnatural scene
> They laugh at. O my mother, mother! O!
> You have won a happy victory to Rome;
> But for your son, believe it, O believe it,
> Most dangerously you have with him prevail'd,
> If not most mortal to him.

And should such an interpretation be considered ridiculous, one has only to remember that Hermione's defence in *The Winter's Tale*, written two years later, opens with the very words with which Blessed Edmund Campion opened his defence and which would be recognised by every Catholic in the audience: 'Since what I am to say must be but that which contradicts my accusation, and the testimony on my part no other but what comes from myself, it shall scarce boot me to say "Not Guilty." '*

Yet, granted William Shakespeare's Catholicism, the question still remains: What kind of a 'Papist' was he? As Dr Magee has shown in his exhaustive and critical enquiry,

* I must record my gratitude to Mrs Martin Hotine for pointing this out to me. It, together with other references, sheds an entirely new light on *The Winter's Tale* and gives a clue which, if patiently followed, may revolutionise the interpretation of the last four plays.

based on contemporary documents, *The English Recusants*,
two-thirds of the population were still Catholic until the
time of the Armada (that is to say, after Shakespeare had
left Stratford for London) and even after 1588, with its
savage anti-Catholic legislation and the pervasive propaganda which stigmatised the Catholics as pro-Spanish
and 'unpatriotic,' the proportion only fell to half by Queen
Elizabeth's death in 1603. The 'Gunpowder Plot' of 1605
led to the even more stringent legislation of 1606, forcing
every known Catholic to commit the final apostasy of
receiving the Anglican sacrament once a year under penalty
of fines beginning (in modern values) at £600 for the first
abstention, £1,200 for the second and £3,600 for every
subsequent time, half the money going to the Crown and
the other half to the informer.

In such a situation, all but the wealthiest or the bravest
were forced into at least an appearance of conformity and
Shakespeare's position was peculiarly vulnerable. He had
already more than once been in trouble for his Catholicism.
He was the cousin of the leading 'Gunpowder Plot' conspirators, Catesby, Tresham, Winter and the Grants. His friend
and patron, the young Earl of Southampton, was an open
Catholic who paid the fines and whose London house had
that same year been raided and 'above two hundred pounds'
worth of Popish books' taken from it and officially burnt in
St Paul's Churchyard.

If Shakespeare outwardly 'conformed' at this period, it
would be neither surprising nor evidence against his continuing Catholicism. Yet there is no evidence that he did
and what evidence there is points the other way, for he
went to live with a Huguenot family who were exempted
from the obligation of attending the Anglican Church. He
thus conveniently 'lost' himself as far as registration was
concerned. Though the names of his fellow-actors are found
in the Southwark token books, proving that they received
Communion according to the law, Shakespeare's name is

not among them; and when he moved to Cripplegate he went to live with Christopher Mountjoy, the Huguenot tiremaker, as one of the family – a family officially outside the net of the recusancy laws. There seems no reason for doubting the conclusion of J. J. Walsh in his *Was Shakespeare a Catholic?* that 'Shakespeare, while in London, so planned his life as to avoid attendance at Anglican services.'

Yet whatever attitude he may have taken outwardly, there is no doubt that, in his spiritual experience, these were his most terrible years. For him, the aftermath of the 'Gunpowder Plot' and the 1606 legislation were *King Lear* and *Timon of Athens*, written in 1606 and 1607; nor does their indictment of 'all men governing' need any explanation in his life but those events and that date.

But to understand the probable nature of his deathbed it is necessary to see something more of his life and work in relation to his Faith, and it is worth noticing that his purchase of New Place in 1597 and his retirement to it in 1611 both coincided with attacks on him for his 'Papist' leanings in regard to one of his greatest creations, Falstaff.

II : The Incubus of Falstaff

THE magnificence of Shakespeare's achievement in creating Falstaff has in part obscured his intention, while the
difference in the theological climate between his age and ours
has rendered almost unintelligible the sharpness of the
original controversy about the character. To this age,
through the work of generations of actors and critics; the fat
knight is an endearing, a-moral figure who justifies the cry
'Banish plump Jack – and banish all the world' and whose
death, 'babbling o' green fields' has provided one of the
immortal passages in the world's literature. Moreover,
Henry V's dismissal of him has come to be regarded as almost
a blot on the character of the hero-king, and A. C. Bradley
in 1902 was constrained to write a lengthy essay to justify
Shakespeare's artistry in allowing the rejection of Falstaff.

In the course of this, Bradley, conditioned by his Protestant
Victorian background, incidentally revealed his own misunderstanding of the matter. He conceded that should an
audience regard Sir John as an old reprobate, not only a
sensualist, a liar and a coward, but a cruel and dangerous
ruffian – all of which Falstaff undoubtedly is – then they
would find no difficulty in accepting as 'good' the King's:

> I have long dreamt of such a kind of man,
> So surfeit-swelled, so old and so profane;
> But, being awaked, I do despise my dream.

On the other hand, the Professor dismissed without discussion
the idea that Shakespeare might have intended such a

reaction on the grounds that 'this idea implies that kind of inability to understand Shakespeare with which it is idle to argue.' But it was Bradley who was mistaken, as he would have discovered had he troubled to examine the facts instead of indulging the curious illusion that he held the key to the dramatist's mind.

That Shakespeare in Falstaff created something very much greater than the caricature of a Lollard hero, no one will deny. From the first, audiences applauded him much as audiences applaud him today and for the same reasons*

> . . . let but Falstaff come,
> Hal, Poins, the rest – you scarce shall have a room,
> All is so pestered . . .

The fact that Falstaff was at first 'Oldcastle' now means less than nothing. But it meant a great deal at the time and the controversy about it echoed for over half a century.

The historical Sir John Oldcastle was, in fact, a companion of Henry V when he was Prince of Wales; he served Henry IV in the Welsh marches and was at the Battle of Shrewsbury. Henry V did his best, both as Prince and King, to convert him from heresy. He failed and, for attacks on the Mass and confession and a declaration that the Pope was anti-Christ, Oldcastle was eventually tried and executed. During Shakespeare's lifetime the Elizabethan Protestant writers had carefully rehabilitated Oldcastle, citing him as a martyr for the 'true religion,' one of the Lollard precursors of the Reformation – which, in his tenets, he undoubtedly was.

In 1597, when Shakespeare first presented *Henry IV*, theological discussion was raging about the Calvinist

---

* Though Professor Dover Wilson has pointed out that he is more popular with men than with women (who tend to dislike him) and that, in the nineteenth century, *Henry IV* was not a popular play. Neither, of course, is it in the twentieth.

interpretation of 'salvation by faith alone.' The sixth of the Lambeth Articles had recently pronounced that 'one who is endued with a justifying faith is certain, with the full assurance of faith, with the remission of his sins and of everlasting salvation' – which meant, in practice, that anyone who was privately convinced that he was of the 'elect' could with impunity commit whatever sins he liked, since his moral conduct, or lack of it, could not possibly prejudice his assured salvation.

In Falstaff, who inveighs scornfully against the 'sons of darkness' and angrily against 'the whore of Babylon' (the Protestant term for the Catholic Church), Shakespeare drew a portrait of one of the more famous of 'the elect.' So that there could be no possible doubt, he called the character 'Sir John Oldcastle' and incorporated some of the actual career of the man who had recently been given popular canonisation by the Protestants.

No one missed the point and Shakespeare was ordered by authority (some say the highest, the Queen herself, at the instance of one of Oldcastle's descendants) at once to change the name. Though he complied, it remained quite obvious who the character was meant to be and traces still linger in the text as we have it.* And, in the substitution of the name 'Falstaff' for 'Oldcastle,' Shakespeare remained, in a certain sense, obdurate; for 'Falstaff' is a thinly disguised version of 'Fastolfe,' another Lollard martyr, whom he had already depicted as a notable coward in *Henry VI*.

The reaction to the play was immediate. A rival company hastily had written and performed a play (the composite work of four authors) entitled *Sir John Oldcastle*, a defence of the Lollard, into which was introduced a Catholic priest, the Parson of Wrotham, who corresponded to Shakespeare's

* In, for example, the Prince's name for Falstaff: 'My old lad of the castle'; in the line: 'Away, good Ned, Falstaff sweats to death,' which will scan only if 'Oldcastle' is substituted for 'Falstaff' and for the retention of the prefix *Old*, before one of Falstaff's speeches.

Falstaff – a glutton, a lecher, a thief, a gambler and a retailer of obscenities, who announced himself:

> A priest in show, but in plain terms a thief
> . . . for what's this life,
> Except the crabbed bitterness thereof
> Be sweetened now and then with lechery?
> I have my Doll, my concubine, as 'twere,
> To frolic with, a lusty, bouncing girl

and so on.

Shakespeare's masterpiece, however, remained, in popular thought, *the* Oldcastle play and when, in 1600, *Sir John Oldcastle* was acted officially at Court, a prologue carefully explained the difference:

> It is no pampered glutton we present,
> Nor aged counsellor to youthful sin,
> But one whose virtue shone above the rest
> . . . Let fair truth be graced,
> Since forged invention former times defaced!

'Forged invention' or not, the controversy continued and in 1603, Fr Robert Persons, SJ, writing a pamphlet, *Of Three Conversions*, under the pseudonym of N.D. (Nicholas Dolman), referred to 'Sir John Oldcastle, a ruffian-knight, as all England knoweth, and commonly brought in by comedians on their stages.'

It was a delayed result of this reference which ultimately in 1611 proved so dangerous to the Shakespeare of the post-'Gunpowder Plot' era that he retired to Stratford to the house he had bought in the year of Falstaff's first appearance and wrote no more. For in 1611 was published John Speed's *History of Great Britain*, in which occurred the following passage: 'N.D., author of the *Three Conversions* hath made Oldcastle a ruffian, a robber and a rebel, and his authority taken from the stage players is more befitting the pen of his slanderous report than the credit of the judicious, being only grounded from this papist and his poet, of like conscience for lies, the one ever feigning, the other falsifying the truth.'*

In the description 'this papist and his poet,' Shakespeare was at last publicly exposed and – who shall blame him? – shrank from the possible consequences of it. He had conquered Caliban in his imagined world, but the monster was master of the real. He wrote no more plays; but retired to New Place to wait for death.

---

* The attacks did not cease with Shakespeare's death. About 1625, Richard James wrote 'the person with which he undertook to play a buffoon was not Falstaff but Sir John Oldcastle and that offence being worthily taken . . . the poet was put to make an ignorant shift of abusing Sir John Fastolfe, a man of not inferior virtue . . . who gave witness unto the truth of our Reformation with a constant and resolute martyrdom, unto which he was pursued by the priests, bishops, monks and friars of those days.' Thomas Fuller in his *Church History* thirty years later made the same point: 'Sir John Falstaff hath relieved the memory of Sir John Oldcastle and, of late, is substituted buffoon in his place; but it matters as little what petulant poets as what malicious papists have written against him.'

III : New Place

WHEN Shakespeare bought New Place for £60 in 1597, it was just over a hundred years old – in disrepair, certainly, and needing much attention, but still 'a pretty house of brick and timber' in the centre of the town and, all things considered, with its wide bay windows, its ornamental gables and its columned doorway, its three-quarters of an acre of garden, its courtyard, its barns, its stables and its orchard, the best house in Stratford.

It had been built at the beginning of Henry VII's reign by the wealthy mercer, Sir Hugh Clopton, a Lord Mayor of London in the 1490's who had spent on Stratford something of his profits. Not only had Sir Hugh fashioned the New Place for his own use and pleasure but he had not been unmindful of the town's civic and religious needs. He had built a new stone bridge to replace the old wooden one, where the lesser roads from London by Oxford and Banbury met; and he had restored and in part rebuilt the Chapel of the Guild of the Holy Cross, a few paces across the road from New Place, which, more than the parish church, was the religious hub of the town.

Already by Clopton's time the Guild was over two hundred years old and famous far beyond the limits of the town. Every eminent Stratfordian was a member as a matter of course; but among those who, wearing their Augustinian hoods, had attended in the Chapel the Requiem Masses sung for the repose of the souls of their departed brethren were many from other districts who had asked admittance

to so celebrated a confraternity. Wealth attended fame. The
Guild owned much property locally. It provided education
at its school, which had been founded in 1295 and which
Clopton had presented with six new scholarships to Oxford
and Cambridge. It gave financial help to its poorer members
and it maintained an almshouse.

New Place stood at the angle of Chapel Street and Chapel
Lane so that a door in the garden wall opened almost
directly on the Guild Chapel itself, whose porch with its
cross and its saints and its gargoyles still faced Shakespeare
as he went in and out on his usual occasions. Except that
the saints had gone. In the century which lay between the
builder of New Place and its most famous tenant, a merciless
revolution had swept the country. The saints had been
hacked from their niches as, inside, the altar had been
desecrated, the ornaments stolen and the paintings on the
walls plastered into oblivion. Seventeen years before William
Shakespeare's birth, the spoilers had laid their hands on
Stratford. All the Chapel endowments, left by generations
of believers, had been confiscated by the Crown and acquired
by avaricious careerists and the school, reorganised on new
doctrinal lines, was forced to break its centuries-old tradition
in education and become a Protestant Grammar School.

It is important, in this connection, to remember that
Edward VI was not the founder of the Grammar Schools
of England but their 'spoiler.' Nearly two hundred Grammar
Schools existed in England before his reign which were,
for the most part, crippled or abolished under him; and
though, of necessity, he reinstituted some of the others, there
was no Grammar School founded within a hundred years
of the beginning of his reign which had not already existed,
like the one at Stratford, as a chantry school. As Professor
Tawney has put it, 'the grammar schools that Edward VI
founded are those which King Edward VI did not destroy.'

The almost total breakdown of education as a result of
the Reformation was so inescapable that a Protestant divine,

preaching before Edward VI, was moved to warn him: 'The decay of students is so great that there are scarce left of every thousand an hundred . . . Your realm (which I am sorry to speak) shall become more barbarous than Scythia.'

The lack of suitable Protestant teachers meant that, in spite of official disapproval, Catholics were still able to staff some of the schools. At Stratford, Shakespeare was taught for a longer time by Catholics than by Protestants. His first master, John Acton, was a Catholic who had to relinquish his post because of his open sympathy with the Rebellion in the North in 1569; after less than two years of the Protestant Walter Roche, Simon Hunt was appointed and taught from Shakespeare's seventh till his eleventh year. In 1575 Hunt decided to become a Catholic priest and left for Douai, taking with him one of the senior boys, Robert Debdale, who also became a priest and who returned to die as a martyr at Tyburn about the time Shakespeare arrived in London.* The name of Hunt's successor is not known, but in 1578 the mastership fell to Thomas Jenkins, an undoubted Protestant, immortalised by Shakespeare as Sir Hugh Evans in *The Merry Wives of Windsor*, who made himself so generally unpopular that within a year he was bribed to resign by money advanced by the Stratford Corporation. His successor was another Catholic, John Cottam, brother of the Thomas Cottam whom Robert Debdale described as 'the two-half of my life' and who, like Debdale, became a priest and returned to martyrdom in England. It was probably on account of Thomas Cottam's execution, since it was in the same year, that his brother retired from the mastership to make way for Alexander Aspinall, who remained in the post for forty-two years and attended Shakespeare's funeral.

When Shakespeare was a boy, trudging unwillingly to

* Shakespeare may have been present at his martyrdom at Tyburn. Whether he was or not seems a more profitable speculation than the conventional query as to whether he held horses outside the theatre.

school from his father's house in Henley Street, New Place, whose gate faced the school playground, was owned by old William Underhill. He died when Shakespeare was six. Underhill's son, also William, inherited New Place together with the other family property at Fillongley and Idlicote; married his first cousin, Mary Underhill, and had eight children. The eldest was mentally defective and murdered his father in 1597, two months after New Place had been sold and before all the legal transactions needful to transfer the property to Shakespeare had been completed. It was not until 1602 that Shakespeare's ownership of New Place was finally confirmed.

But it was not the sharp scarlet of the personal tragedy so much as the grey monotone of daily pressures which gave New Place its tragic setting. For William Underhill was a stubborn Catholic who refused to attend Anglican services on Sundays and had, by law, to pay for the privilege. What this meant, in terms of mounting poverty and increasing danger, the dates themselves sufficiently indicate to those familiar with the Elizabethan landscape. As few aids to understanding are more freely neglected than dates, it is permissible to remind the reader of some relevant occurrences between 1570, when William Underhill Senior died and Shakespeare was six, and 1597, when William Underhill Junior was murdered and Shakespeare, aged 33, bought New Place for £60 in the currency of the time.

Few things are more difficult than the calculation of a genuine equivalent of former prices. Today (1961) in England money is worth less than a third of what it was in 1939: that is to say, a pound then would buy what costs rather more than three pounds now; and the 1939 value is, at most, half of that in 1901. An income of £150 a year at the end of Queen Victoria's reign would mean more, in purchasing power and comfort, than an income of £1,250 at the beginning of Elizabeth II's. It is generally accepted that the value of mid-sixteenth-century money was one-

twentieth of that at the beginning of the nineteenth century –
'a halfpenny of Henry VII's money was equal in value to
tenpence of Pitt's' – so that, even assuming (to be very safely
conservative in our estimate) that the value of money in
relation to goods remained stable throughout the whole
of the nineteenth century to the beginning of the twentieth,
from Pitt to Asquith, one would have to multiply by sixty
Elizabethan values to get the modern equivalent. That this
is roughly accurate may be deduced from the fact that the
£60 Shakespeare paid for New Place would be about £3,600,
which represents a bargain price for an equivalent house
in the country today.

In modern currency, it was possible for Catholics in the
early years of Queen Elizabeth I's reign to purchase the
right of exemption from attending Anglican services on
Sundays for about £160 a year; though even this, where
with the children and the servants there was a family of
twelve – an average Catholic household – meant the expen-
diture of about £2,000 a year. And as the reign proceeded
conditions deteriorated.

In 1571 any Catholic obtaining rosaries or crucifixes
from abroad (and there was no other way of obtaining them
except through travellers from the Continent) was made
subject to the confiscation of all his goods as well as imprisonment. In 1581 anyone who made or became a convert
to Catholicism was made subject to the penalties of high
treason – hanging, drawing and quartering. In 1585 Catholics were forbidden to send their children abroad to receive
Catholic education, while any who did not inform the local
authorities of the whereabouts of Catholic priests were to be
fined and imprisoned at the Queen's pleasure. In 1587,
the fines for non-attendance at Anglican services were
increased to £600 a month (in modern values) which must
be paid within six months – at each Easter and Michaelmas –
under the penalty of confiscation of all the goods and half
of all the landed property of the offender. In 1593 this was

tightened so that any over sixteen absenting themselves
from the Anglican church might be imprisoned. To ensure
effective surveillance, no Catholic was allowed to move
more than five miles from his home under pain of confiscation
of all his goods, chattels and – for his lifetime – lands.

It was this last attack which broke William Underhill
who, though crippled with fines, had managed, by main-
taining three establishments – at Idlicote, at Fillongley and
at Stratford – to evade some of the rigours of the law. It
was, indeed, precisely at such people as Underhill, who
continued as 'stubborn recusants' and by having more than
one place of residence managed to substantiate doubts as to
where they were on any given Sunday, that the Act was
aimed. Stratford was more than five miles from Idlicote,
which was the centre of the Underhill property; for years
there had been no spare money to keep New Place even
in repair. By 1597 it had become a useless burden, to be
disposed of thankfully to Shakespeare, in London with
Falstaff.

And in selling it to him, Underhill was disposing of it to a
friend. The idea indeed may have originated not with either
of the Williams but with the poet's father, John Shakespeare,
who, like William Underhill, was a 'stubborn recusant'
ruined by fines. The Stratford tradesman and the Warwickshire landowner were caught alike in the same net; and
between all Catholics, thus facing death or economic ruin
as an alternative to apostasy, were forged unbreakable
bonds.

IV : Sir Thomas Lucy and the Shakespeares

THE Puritan Sir Thomas Lucy, that 'vain, weak and vindictive magistrate' (as Oldys described him) was, in his hatred of Catholics, the ideal instrument of Government policy in Warwickshire. From his mansion at Charlecote, four miles from Stratford, he was the mainspring of the drive against papistry from the mid-seventies onward. In 1576 a Grand Commission Ecclesiastical had been appointed to enquire into the administration of the anti-Catholic laws and in the summer of 1577 a move was made by Whitgift, the Anglican Bishop of Worcester, shortly to be made Archbishop of Canterbury where his inaugural sermon was on his favourite theme: 'The Pope is Anti-Christ.' Whitgift, finding his own clergy remiss in reporting recusants, conferred with Sir Thomas Lucy over the 'discipline' of 'that part of Warwickshire which is in my diocese,' emphasising particularly the requirements of the government that he was to 'order, correct, reform and punish any persons wilfully and obstinately absenting themselves from church and service,' and that he was to report not only the names of the recusants but 'the value of their land and goods, as he shall think they are, not as they are given in the subsidy book.'

Ecclesiastical permission to persecute to the limit, without regard to the facts of the case, was backed up by a secular Commission for the musters, which suggested that force was to be used if necessary; and in the October of 1577, Sir Thomas Lucy, as one of the Commissioners, arrived

28

officially in Stratford to make his formal investigation. The result of it was sent by Whitgift to the Privy Council: 'I have set down the names of such as by common report are noted to be great mislikers of the religion now professed and do absent themselves from the Church, with values of their lands and goods as they are thought to be by the common voice and opinion; most earnestly beseeching Your Honours, even for God's sake, to provide some discipline for them lest others, by their example, fall to the like contempt.' Prominent among them was Sir Robert Throckmorton, father-in-law of Edward Arden, head of William Shakespeare's mother's house; grandfather of Robert Catesby and Francis Tresham; great-uncle of the three Winters and John Grant – boys who were later to be six of the 'Gunpowder Plot' conspirators.

In the January of 1578, further action was taken. A levy was made in Stratford for the strengthening of the militia to be used in enforcing the anti-Catholic measures and preventing possible riots. John Shakespeare, assessed at 3s. 4d., refused to pay. What is more, meeting force with cunning, the 'merry-cheeked old man' decided to save what was left of his property by parting with it to friends on privately-understood terms. He and his wife, Mary Arden, leased 86 acres of land in Wilmcote in perpetuity to two of their friends, provided that a trusted Catholic neighbour could live there for twenty-one years on the annual payment of a quarter of wheat and a quarter of barley. Other property they mortgaged or sold to relatives.

Hardly were these transactions completed than Sir Thomas Lucy appeared again, this time to make a list of 'freeholders and gentlemen' for taxable purposes and militia service. John Shakespeare, who remained obdurate, was committed for 'a breach of the Queen's peace' and fined £20 for non-appearance to answer the charge. At the same time – the spring of 1580 – his last child, Edmund, William's third and youngest brother, was born and duly baptized in the parish church by the Anglican clergyman.

In the matter of baptisms (which, provided correct form and matter are used, are valid even if administered by those not in Holy Orders) the Shakespeares, like other Catholics in Stratford, were content to use the Parish Church. In the matter of marriages, however, where it was practicable, recusants preferred to get a special licence for a wedding at Temple Grafton, a village near Stratford, which had still for its parish-priest a Catholic, Father John Frith (the original of Shakespeare's Friar Laurence in *Romeo and Juliet*).

'Old Father John' was one of the few priests who had managed to continue in office under the Elizabethan government. He was despised by the Anglicans because he could not preach well and he was not feared, by reason of his age and his harmless goodness, by authority. This, combined with the difficulty in finding Anglican clergy (Elizabeth, when told that 40,000 sound clergy were needed for her churches, remarked wisely: 'Forty thousand! Jesu, it is not to be looked for!') accounted for the immunity of Father Frith, who, nevertheless, was entered in the official records as 'unsound in religion.' And there, at Temple Grafton, William Shakespeare, aged eighteen and a half, was married to the twenty-six-year-old Anne Hathaway in the November of 1582.

It was the natural place for any Stratford Catholic to be married, but whether it was the young man's own spontaneous choice or whether it needed the urging of his uncompromising parents, there is no means of knowing. Many people think that there is an echo of the circumstance in *As You Like It* and that what Jaques says to Touchstone in warning him against marriage by the Anglican Martext is what John Shakespeare said to William when the latter was prepared to be married by the Anglican vicar of Stratford: 'Get you to church and have a good priest that can tell you what marriage is: this fellow will not join you as they join wainscot; then one of you will prove a shrunk panel and, like green timber, warp, warp!'

It may have been so. The words have the ring of John Shakespeare. But what is certain is that William had to pay heavily for the privilege of a Catholic marriage. When the licence was granted he had to guarantee the sum of forty pounds to Whitgift for allowing it – or, as the document has it – to 'defend and save harmless the right reverend Father-in-God, Lord John, Bishop of Worcester, and his officers for licensing them, the said William and Anne, to be married together.' When a licence bore no indication of the church or of the officiating clergyman's name, it was tacitly understood that the marriage would be a Catholic one. To demand so great a sum as £40 (in the currency of the time) was in line with Whitgift's persecuting policy and it is significant that three weeks later the sum demanded for such licences was raised to £100 which made them prohibitive to all but the wealthiest.

The year after the marriage, the Shakespeares found themselves compromised by a Catholic 'plot.' John Somerville, a near neighbour, owner of the manor of Edreston, had married their cousin, the daughter of Edward Arden. He was about William Shakespeare's age, but was slightly unbalanced and the penal measures against Catholics had made him fall into melancholia. Like his other cousins Catesby, Winter, Tresham and the rest who were later to organise the 'Gunpowder Plot,' he saw in violence the remedy for oppression. He decided to kill the Queen as the fount of all Catholic troubles. Eluding his family, he set off for London proclaiming his intention to shoot her and set her head on a pole, as she had recently set those of many martyrs, including Blessed Edmund Campion. Somerville was, needless to say, speedily arrested and thrown into the Tower of London. Edward Arden, realising that all his family would be involved, endeavoured to save at least his private chaplain, Father Hugh Hall – who lived with them disguised as a gardener – by sending him over to William Underhill at Idlicote.

But it was of no avail. At last the Government had got something concrete to expand into one of its 'plots.' On October 31, 1583, a warrant was issued for the arrest of 'such as shall be in any way akin to all touched, and to search their houses.' On November 2, Thomas Wilkes, Clerk to the Privy Council, arrived at Charlecote, and for fifteen days he and Sir Thomas Lucy investigated the affair with the thoroughness of hate and fanaticism. Lucy went personally to arrest Edward Arden, his wife Mary and his brother Francis. Somerville's wife and sister and Father Hugh Hall were also sent to London for trial and death or imprisonment. But other Catholics had had time to hide the evidences of their faith and Wilkes wrote testily to the Secretary of State: 'In all the houses of the papists in which we have made search, although most of them are known to be very notorious papists, we have not found either books, letters or any show of popery, beads, crosses or other trumperies that might draw them into suspicion: which hath been prevented by conveying away from their houses all such things, immediately upon the rumour of the apprehension of Somerville.' Then, with a euphemistic invitation to torture, he added: 'Unless you can make Somerville, Arden, Hall the priest, Somerville's wife and his sister to speak directly to those things which you desire to have discovered, it will not be possible for us here to find out more than is to be found already, for the Papists in this country (i.e. Warwickshire) greatly do work upon the advantage of clearing their houses of all shows of suspicion.'

What John Shakespeare had in particular to conceal was the 'Spiritual Will' which lay undiscovered under the roof-tiles of his Henley Street house till 1757 when a bricklayer, retiling the western part of the house, brought it accidentally to light. It may be that William himself, who lived in the house and was presumably more agile than his father, put it there.

The 'Spiritual Will' was a particular form of confession of

faith designed for times of persecution. It was popularised by St Charles Borromeo, the great Archbishop of Milan, who died in 1584. He himself composed the standard text in Italian, Spanish and French. The English version may have been translated by Father Persons or by his companion on the English Mission, Blessed Edmund Campion. Both of them visited St Charles in 1580 on their way to England and (for Campion) death; and in a letter sent by Cardinal Allen, who was in charge of English affairs, to the English College in Rome in 1581 was the message: 'We have heard from England by a letter from Father Robert Persons, SJ, that the persecution still rages with the same fury . . . Fr Robert wants three or four thousand more of the testaments, for many people desire to have them.'

The title of these documents was: 'The Testament or Last Will of the Soul, made in health for the Christian to secure himself from the temptations of the devil at the hour of death.' The Testament could be copied by the testator in his own handwriting or merely have his signature on a printed copy. In either case, it represented, in a very real sense, the true 'will' of one who, under persecution and torture, might find his body unequal to the demands of his soul. Nothing more appropriate could have been found for the ordinary English Catholic of those times; if it was a 'little' heroism, it was still heroism to sign and keep it; and it says much for John Shakespeare's courage that, even in that moment of extreme danger, he did not burn the incriminating evidence which, had Sir Thomas Lucy discovered it, might well have sent him to London, where in due course Edward Arden was hanged, drawn and quartered and his head set on London Bridge; Somerville was murdered in prison the day before Arden's execution, and his head set up beside Arden's; Mary Arden was condemned to be burnt, but was reprieved and with her daughter, Somerville's wife, and with Father Hall, sentenced to a long term of imprisonment.

B

The absence of evidence against the Shakespeares, however, as definitely of those 'in any way kin' to the Ardens,
did not save them from arrest and questioning. There seems
little doubt that this was the period when Sir Thomas Lucy
had William Shakespeare 'oft whipped and sometimes
imprisoned and at last made him fly his native country to
his great advancement.'

The suggestion that the punishment was for deer-stealing
in Sir Thomas Lucy's park has been discredited since the
discovery that Lucy had no park to steal deer from or to
poach in. The story may have arisen from a misapplication
of the situation in *The Merry Wives of Windsor* or it may have
been the 'cover' by which Shakespeare's descendants
shielded from the world the true reason. Both Davies and
Rowe, who tell the story, could have consulted Shakespeare's
granddaughter – and, indeed, may have done so – but the
last thing she would have wanted known in the reign of
William III, just after the complete triumph of Protestantism
in 1688, would be the Catholicism of the Shakespeares.

For whatever reason, William departed to the relative
anonymity of London, but his father remained in Stratford,
staunch in his recusancy, persecuted but militant, till his
death in 1601 – the year his son wrote *Hamlet* with its tribute
to a father who

> was a man, take him for all in all
> We shall not look upon his like again.

John had written in his 'Spiritual Will' twenty years earlier:
'I John Shakespeare do protest that I will pass out of this
life, armed with the last sacrament of Extreme Unction,
the which, if through any let or hindrance I should not then
be able to have, I do also for that time demand and crave
the same, beseeching His Divine Majesty that He will be
pleased to anoint my senses both internal and external
with the sacred oil of His infinite mercy . . .'

Whether some secret priest was able to administer Unction

or whether the sacrament remained 'of desire' there is no means of knowing. By the turn of the century, the persecution had reached new heights and in 1595 Sir Thomas Lucy had achieved a local triumph. At Alvechurch Place, a few miles from Stratford, the home of the Catholic Dorothy Heath, a priest who had been resident there – in disguise – had been discovered, arrested and, in due course, hanged, drawn and quartered at Warwick. It was intended to terrorize the Catholics of the neighbourhood, though Lucy must have resented Father Freeman's public snub when, as he continued to pester him with the key question: 'Is the Queen Supreme Head of the Church?' the priest, with a few hours to live, merely turned away with: 'I have other matters now to answer to.'

Since then it is likely that Catholics took even greater care not to endanger the lives of their hunted priests, and with Lucy's spies on the watch and John Shakespeare's recusancy so well known, the old man may have been content with what he had expressed in his Spiritual Will. But at least it is not possible to doubt that he craved the Sacraments and died, as he had lived, in the faith of 'the one Holy Catholic Apostolic Roman Church.'

V : Events of 1601

ONE of the more curious assumptions made about Shakespeare's life is that, because he left Stratford in the fifteen-eighties and did not retire to it till 1611, he never visited it in the interim. For some critics, Stratford might be the Antipodes instead of a country town within easy reach of London and as accessible then as it is now. There is no reason to suppose that the poet was not at his father's death-bed – the more so as we know that from the spring to the Christmas of 1601 his company was not in the capital, but touring in an enforced 'rustication.' The public events of 1601 had enmeshed Shakespeare no less than his private grief. For it was the year of the abortive Essex rising.

The full story and implications of that episode have not yet been fully elucidated by historians, but the main lines of it are clear. The Earl of Essex, thirty-three years younger than the Queen and the object of her sexagenarian sensuality, was secretly in correspondence with James of Scotland whose succession to the English throne he was, at the end of the sixteenth century, prepared to secure, if necessary by armed insurrection. Though Essex himself was a Protestant, he had for two reasons persuaded many Catholics to join him. In the first place, James had promised toleration to Catholics; in the second, the Queen's ministers, Cecil and Raleigh (for the moment acting together against Essex whose influence with Elizabeth menaced them both) were the real objects of attack; and the displacement of Cecil, the

36

architect of persecution, was a commendable Catholic objective. James and Essex, even if they subsequently broke their word,* could hardly be worse than Elizabeth and Cecil.

The chief of the Catholic conspirators was the young Earl of Southampton, Shakespeare's friend and patron, who hero-worshipped Essex and who, with another Catholic, Sir Christopher Blount, Essex's stepfather, had accompanied him to Ireland. Others included Catesby, Winter and Tresham as well as Sir Charles Percy and Sir Jocelyn Percy. Shakespeare was thus doubly involved, through his patron and through his cousins. But, on the eve of the rebellion, he was drawn even closer.

On Saturday, February 7, 1601, Sir Gelly Meyrick, Essex's steward, dined at Gunter's with Monteagle, Blount, the Percies, Tresham, Edward Bushell (a member of the 'cousinage' and a militant Catholic suspected by the Government), Sir John Davis (also a Catholic) and several others. The Catholic nature of this gathering was later stressed by Cecil's accusation at Essex's trial that Essex himself was a secret Catholic: 'Indeed your religion appears by Blount, Davis and Tresham, and by your promising liberty of conscience hereafter.' After dinner they crossed the river to the Globe Theatre to witness a special performance of Shakespeare's *Richard II*.

This had been arranged the previous day by Sir Gelly Meyrick and Henry Cuffe, Essex's sardonic secretary, who had eventually overcome the reluctance of the company's manager, Augustine Phillips, by promising to double the actors' fees and giving Phillips himself forty shillings in gold. The ostensible reason for the manager's original refusal was that *Richard II* was an old play and that no one would patronise it. As it happened the Globe was crowded, but, in

* As James, of course, when he eventually came to the English throne did, with the memorable observation: 'Na, na, we'll no need the Papists noo.'

any case, no one could have misunderstood that the extra fee was not so much a box-office guarantee as 'danger-money.' *Richard II*, in the best of circumstances, was a risk for political reasons. When it had been published in 1597, the censor had insisted on the excision of the deposition scene. In 1599 an unfortunate historian, John Hayward, who had written a life of Henry IV and dedicated it to Essex, was put in prison for it and left there for the rest of the reign. The Queen herself was under no misapprehension about the intended parallel between Henry Bolingbroke's deposition of Richard and Essex's wishful deposition of her. Later that year, 1601, she remarked with some emphasis: 'I am Richard II' and pointed out that Shakespeare's tragedy had been 'played forty times in the open streets and houses' – which hardly supports Augustine Phillips's suggestion of unpopularity. At the same time his hesitation and his additional payment of forty shillings in gold were comprehensible enough. He played Bolingbroke.

There was, thereafter, on that Saturday afternoon no question of the dangerous topicality of the play. John of Gaunt's dying speech to Richard was uncomfortably apposite to the Queen and the Cecil party:

> Thy death-bed is no lesser than thy land,
> Wherein thou liest in reputation sick;
> And thou, too careless patient as thou art,
> Commit'st they anointed body to the care
> Of those physicians that first wounded thee.

Nor would the Catholics in the audience miss the undertones of the reference to the mediaeval monarchy of England – the Catholic kings

> Fear'd by their breed and famous by their birth,
> Renowned for their deeds as far from home,
> For Christian service and true chivalry,
> As is the sepulchre in stubborn Jewry

Of the world's ransom, Blessed Mary's Son;
This land of such dear souls, this dear dear land,
Dear for her reputation through the world,
Is now leased out – I die pronouncing it –
Like to a tenement or pelting farm!

The part of John of Gaunt was, presumably, played by
Shakespeare himself who, at least until 1603, ordinarily acted
those 'old men's parts' like Adam in *As You Like It* and the
Ghost in *Hamlet* which – in Ivor Brown's words – 'would
not be too exacting and would provide leisure to watch and
shape the greater part of the rehearsal.' In any case Shakespeare was inextricably bound, through no fault of his own,
to the rebellion which broke out next day when his cousin,
Catesby, as always a miracle of courage, led the last des-
pairing fight in the Strand and for which his beloved patron,
Southampton, was in due course condemned to death for
high treason.*

The execution of Essex was fixed for Ash Wednesday,
February 25. On the evening of the 24th, the writ of execution
was sent to the Tower. Then, suddenly, the Queen sent an
order countermanding it and settled down to enjoy the
customary Shrovetide play. The players chosen were, with
malicious irony, the same who had acted *Richard II* nearly
three weeks earlier (Phillips had been examined by the
Privy Council on February 18) and when their performance
was over, the Queen retired to her private apartments and
sent another message to the Tower, ordering the execution
to take place as planned.

It is unfortunate that literary criticism and history are
so kept in water-tight compartments that Sir Edmund
Chambers can write of this performance merely as an

---

* Southampton, as a result of Essex's passionate plea for him, was
spared death, but was imprisoned with such rigour for the rest of the
reign that the Lieutenant of the Tower eventually refused to be responsible of the consequences unless he was granted 'more air, more exercise
and spiritual comfort.'

argument that the Company was not punished by being sent on a long provincial tour. He says that it is not clear that that journeying was due to the performance of *Richard II* since 'the company was at Court on 24 February 1601, only a fortnight after the Essex affair.' He seems unaware of the implications of the date. Though no record of the play chosen for performance can be found, the circumstance that the Queen had reprieved Essex before she saw it and ordered his execution after she had seen it suggests that it must have been *Richard II* – which would also account for the fact that, in the August of that year, she spoke of it with such vehemence.

The historical possibility of Shakespeare on that occasion playing John of Gaunt before the Queen, four years after her anger about Oldcastle-Falstaff, gives a truer picture of the probable relationship between them than the legends invented later in conformity with the convention that the 'great' necessarily appreciate one another. It is just possible that the story of *The Merry Wives of Windsor* being written in deference to Elizabeth's desire to see Falstaff in love* may have some foundation in fact but the alleged interchange of courtesies over the Queen's dropped glove when Shakespeare was acting a king on the stage – which first made its appearance in 1825 – has long been abandoned.

The most important comment on the feelings of a Catholic dramatist for the two persecuting sovereigns under whom he lived is that, at a time when his fellow-writers were most fulsomely eulogistic, 'no dirge for Elizabeth or paean for James' – as Chambers expresses it – 'came from his pen.'

But in this same year, 1601, there was published the most

---

* Though not printed till 1602, the play was probably written and performed in the winter of 1591–2. It thus preceded the offending Oldcastle-Falstaff of *Henry IV* (as the internal literary evidence also suggests) and, as T. W. Baldwin in his monumental *The Organization and Personnel of the Shakespearean Company* (1927) puts it: 'It was probably the *Henry VI* Fastolfe instead of the *Henry IV* Falstaff that Queen Elizabeth wanted to see in love, if indeed there is any truth at all in the old tradition.'

mysterious of Shakespeare's writings which has been, by
one school of critics, wrongly associated with the Queen.
It was a poem, one of a collection to which several writers,
including Ben Jonson, contributed on the set theme of
'The Phoenix and the Turtle.' The dedicatee was Sir John
Salusbury. In 1601, Salusbury was 34. Through his mother
he was descended from an illegitimate son of Henry VII;
his wife was an illegitimate daughter of the fourth
Earl of Derby. He married her in 1586, when he was
nineteen. That year was the crucial one in his life. His
elder brother, Thomas, was executed for his part in the
Babington 'Plot,' protesting on the scaffold: 'I have lived a
Catholic and so will die.' According to all accounts, John
was deeply affected by his brother's tragic end, though at
some unknown date after this he seems to have apostasised.
That date seems to be about the Christmas of 1600. A friend
in Gray's Inn had that year warned him to change 'the
lion's skin with the fox, for it is better for his age,' adding:
'Molehills must think they are trodden down, if mountains be
pulled down.' At any rate, John, in the Essex affair, carefully espoused Cecil's side and got his knighthood for it later
in the year. His cousin, Captain Owen Salusbury, was
however the first casualty on Essex's side; and another
John Salusbury, also his relative, was a Jesuit engaged on
the English Mission. How far Sir John's apostasy was genuine,
it is difficult to tell for in 1606, after the new legislation
making it incumbent on all magistrates to receive the
Anglican sacrament, there is a letter extant urging him to
'go to church' lest he be taken for a Papist.

In 1913 Carleton Brown in his introduction to *Poems by
Sir John Salusbury and Robert Chester* provided an excellent
short biography which may now be supplemented by
reference to the *Calendar of Salusbury Correspondence 1553-c.1700*,
published in 1954. Despite these, however, little light is
thrown on Shakespeare's *The Phoenix and the Turtle* and
Carleton Brown's considered opinion remains valid: 'To

reconcile Shakespeare's allegory either with *Love's Martyr* or with the other poetical essays is manifestly impossible . . . His lines on the Phoenix and the Turtle were a matter of courteous compliance rather than a tribute to a personal friend.'

As long ago as 1875 Emerson wrote of this poem: 'I should like to have the Academy of Letters propose a prize for an essay on Shakespeare's poem *Let the bird of loudest lay* and the *Threnos* with which it closes, the aim of the essay being to explain, by a historical research into the poetic myths and tendencies of the age in which it was written, the frame and allusions of the poem.' Yet, despite over eighty years of patient research on these lines, little has been contributed except somewhat strained metaphysical ingenuities.

Halliwell-Phillips rightly pointed out that the problem was not to be settled by regarding it merely as an allegory of a spiritual union without reference to the personal circumstances. Sir Israel Gollancz believed that 'the private family history of Sir John Salusbury ought to yield the necessary clue to the events' but was not enamoured of Dr Grosart's suggestion that Shakespeare's 'Phoenix' was meant to be Queen Elizabeth and the 'Turtle Dove' typified 'the brilliant but impetuous, the greatly-dowered but rash, the illustrious but unhappy Robert Devereux, second Earl of Essex.'

As Elizabeth was still alive when the poem was written, as the point of Shakespeare's *The Phoenix and the Turtle* is that both of them were dead, and as Salusbury got his knighthood for taking the anti-Essex side, Grosart's interpretation is hardly convincing. Yet, wrong though he is in his identification, he is right in his understanding that there were people to identify and that they were connected with Essex's rebellion.

Two days after Essex's execution, Sir Christopher Blount was beheaded, while at Tyburn, Sir Gelly Meyrick and Richard Cuffe were hanged, drawn and quartered. With them suffered, presumably to impress on the public mind the connection between Papistry and sedition, a Benedictine

and a Jesuit, condemned for their priesthood, and a gentle-
woman, Anne Lyne, guilty of harbouring priests.

The identification of Anne Lyne with Shakespeare's
'Phoenix' was first made by the Countess de Chambrun in
her *Shakespeare Retrouvé* in 1947 (the English translation,
entitled *Shakespeare: A Portrait Restored* was published in
England in 1957). To this Elizabethan authority, who spent
forty years of research on Shakespeare and his background
before writing her masterpiece, this conclusion appeared
'incontrovertible.' Emerson's question was answered. Certainly, once the historical circumstances are understood,
the identification makes the meaning of the poem clear
enough. It also explains why a poem concerned with the
mystical paradox that complete union can, by Divine love,
be achieved between creatures of different essence, different
sex and different species, should, on the one hand, have been
denounced as 'seditious' and, on the other, have been
popular enough, despite the handicap of clandestine publication, to go into a second edition. If the point of it was less
immediately obvious than the performance of *Richard II*, it
was easily comprehensible as a requiem-panegyric for a
martyrdom which, at that time and in that place, was 'not
done in a corner.'

Since the poem is short and not perhaps as well-known as,
for example, the sonnets and the songs from the plays, it
may be as well to print it in full:

> Let the bird of loudest lay,
>   On the sole Arabian tree,
>   Herald sad and trumpet be,
> To whose sound chaste wings obey.
>
> But thou shrieking harbinger,
>   Foul precurrer of the fiend,
>   Augur of the fever's end,
> To this troop come thou not near!

From this session interdict
   Every fowl of tyrant wing,
   Save the eagle, feathered king:
Keep the obsequy so strict.

Let the priest in surplice white,
   That defunctive music can,
   Be the death-divining swan,
Lest the requiem lack his right.

And thou treble-dated crow,
   That thy sable gender makest
   With the breath thou giv'st and takest
'Mongst our mourners shalt thou go.

Here the anthem doth commence:
   Love and constancy is dead;
   Phoenix and the turtle fled
In a mutual flame from hence.

So they lov'd, as love in twain
   Had the essence but in one:
   Two distincts, division none:
Number there in love was slain.

Hearts remote, yet not asunder
   Distance, and no space was seen
   Twixt the turtle and his queen:
But in them it were a wonder.

So between them love did shine
   That the turtle saw his right
   Flaming in the phoenix' sight;
Either was the other's mine.

Property was thus appalled,
   That the self was not the same;
   Single nature's double name
Neither two nor one was called.

Reason, in itself confounded,
  Saw division grow together,
  To themselves yet either neither,
Simple were so well compounded;

That it cried, How true a twain
  Seemeth this concordant one!
  Love hath reason, reason none
If what parts can so remain.

Whereupon it made this threne
  To the phoenix and the dove,
  Co-supremes and stars of love,
As chorus to their tragic scene.

Threnos

Beauty, truth and rarity,
Grace in all simplicity,
Here enclos'd in cinders lie.

Death is now the phoenix' nest;
And the turtle's loyal breast
To eternity doth rest,

Leaving no posterity:
'Twas not their infirmity,
It was married chastity.

Truth may seem, but cannot be;
Beauty brag, but 'tis not she;
Truth and beauty buried be.

To this urn let those repair
That are either true or fair;
For these dead birds sigh a prayer.

Anne Lyne was the daughter of William Higham of
Dunmow in Essex, whose wealth came from plundered
church property and who, comprehensibly enough, was a

strict Anglican. When Anne and her elder brother became Catholics, he disinherited them both, selling his estate so that the son should not inherit and withholding the dowry from the daughter.

Anne married Roger Lyne, a convert like herself who had also been disinherited by his father. When Roger was in Newgate for his recusancy, his father sent him a message from his death-bed asking him to conform and go to an Anglican church for once; otherwise he would have to surrender his inheritance to his younger brother. Roger replied: 'If I must give up either God or the world, I prefer to give up the world.'

After his marriage, he was forced to go to Flanders where he managed to exist on a small pension from Spain, part of which he sent to Anne. On his death, she was left destitute and eventually became housekeeper to the Jesuit, Father John Gerard, who left on record: 'She was just the sort of person I wanted to manage the money matters, take care of the guests and meet the inquiries of strangers. She had good store of charity and wariness, and in great patience she possessed her soul.'

Her wariness, however, deserted her on the Feast of the Purification when she let in so many Catholics to her house to hear Mass that her neighbours became suspicious and called the constables. She had by this time left Fr Gerard because, as he wrote, 'so many people knew who she was that her being in a place was enough to render it unsafe for me. So a room was hired for her in another person's house, where she often used to harbour priests.' Nor, had she still been with him would she have committed her indiscretion. To let in sufficient Catholics to attract the attention of neighbours was 'a thing she would never have done in my house. Good soul, she was more careful of me than of herself.'

When the constables forced an entry, they found Mass in progress and all were arrested. Months later, when Anne

Lyne was brought to trial on the charge of harbouring and
supporting priests, she made no direct answer to the question
of 'Guilty or Not Guilty?' but cried out in a voice that all
could hear: 'My lords, nothing grieves me but that I could
not receive a thousand more!' But she was so weak that she
had to be carried to court in a chair and was perforce
allowed to sit during the trial. The verdict was a foregone
conclusion, but she was not at once executed and it seemed
possible that she might die in prison. This she had always
foreseen and had told Fr Gerard: 'Naturally I want more
than anything to die for Christ, though it is too much to
hope that it will be at the hand of the executioner. Possibly
Our Lord will let me be taken in the same house as a priest
and put in some cold, filthy dungeon, where I shall not last
long.'

She was so weak and the February day was so bitterly
cold when at last she was taken to Tyburn that it seemed
to some that, even at that last moment, she might cheat the
gallows. One bystander noticed that she was so emaciated
that her limbs were thinner than the rope round her neck.
With her were a Jesuit priest, Father Roger Filcock, who,
according to Fr Gerard 'had often been her confessor and had
always been her friend,' and Father Mark Barkworth, a
young Benedictine, who, after his condemnation had walked
through the streets, fettered though he was, with an air of
such magnanimity that the crowd took him for one of the
ringleaders of the Essex rebellion until he explained that
he 'was a soldier of Christ about to die for his faith.'

At the gallows Anne Lyne repeated what she had said at
her trial: 'I am sentenced to die for harbouring a Catholic
priest, and so far from repenting for having done so, I wish
with all my soul that where I have entertained one I could
have entertained a thousand.' She knelt and kissed the
gallows and remained so absorbed in prayer as not to
notice the hangman's hand on her throat. Before her body
was cut down, Fr Barkworth, whose turn was next, pushed

the executioner aside and embraced her, dead, calling out: 'O blessed Mrs Lyne, who hast now happily received thy reward! Thou hast gone before us but we shall, if it please God, quickly follow thee to bliss.' Fr Filcock, reserved till last that the spectacle of the two deaths might a little break his spirit, showed no sign of terror, but only prayed that 'he too might be quickly dissolved in Christ.'

Father Garnet, whose dangerous duty it was to be at every Catholic execution, purchased Anne Lyne's body from the executioner and it was carried off by her friends to some place of burial in a cellar near some church or chapel where, according to Fr Garnet, Catholic burials were always held at midnight.

This, as the Countess de Chambrun says, 'was the event which inspired Shakespeare's immortal allegory. Although pronounced enigmatic, it is in reality simplicity itself.'

It was not so far a cry from Anne Lyne's hurried, hidden funeral in the February snow to John Shakespeare's death and burial in Stratford in the early days of September. It was part of the cruelty of persecution that even the martyrs, although they were dying openly for the Faith, had to forego the ministrations of a priest, unless there happened to be one among the condemned. But for any Papist, open or secret, martyr or conformist or coward, to be deprived of the consolations of religion, sharpens the sting of death. Anne Lyne was fortunate in that her friend and confessor, Fr Roger Filcock, was her co-martyr. Yet even she was not spared the Anglican ministers. As Fr Gerard recorded it: 'Being arrived at the place of punishment, some preachers wanted to tease her, as usual, with warnings to abandon her errors; but she cut them short saying: 'Away! I have no dealings or communion with you!'

The indulging of such honesty was the privilege of the martyr. And, since such occasions were public and known, martyrs were ensured of the prayers of all the faithful in the city as a guerdon of strength at that moment. But the

ordinary Catholic dying had no such consolation and, for
his family's sake, had often, even then, to disguise his religion
and suffer the presence of an Anglican clergyman when
what he most desperately craved was absolution and unction
from a Catholic priest. He could not even ask for prayers
on his soul's journey and there is special poignancy in the
last lines of Shakespeare's final farewell to the stage:

> And my ending is despair
> Unless I be relieved by prayer
> Which pierces so that it assaults
> Mercy itself and frees all faults.
> As you from crimes would pardoned be,
> Let your indulgence set me free!

The death of John Shakespeare must have turned his
son's thoughts more than ever to such matters. Some time
after it, William handed to the manager of the company his
rather untidy manuscript of *Hamlet* and thereafter took no
interest either in its revision or in its production.* With its
spectacle of surrounding corruption driving a sensitive mind
to the edge of suicide, resisted only because of belief in
judgment after death, it stands, underneath its universality,
as Shakespeare's particular memorial of the events of 1601.

A tradition that he wrote the Ghost scenes at his house
in Stratford (that is to say, the Henley Street house where
his father had died: his ownership of New Place had not
yet been legally confirmed) becomes, in the circumstances,
more worthy of credence than it does as a piece of isolated
gossip. There is very good evidence that he himself not
only played the Ghost but that it was in that part that he
was at his best as an actor – that it was the 'top' of his
performance. It is also to be noticed that the part of the
Ghost, as every producer knows, has a kind of disproportion

---

* See Dover Wilson: *The Manuscript of Shakespeare's 'Hamlet'* (1934), a
monumental piece of fieldwork in Shakespearean studies, worth libraries
of 'literary' criticism.

which makes it sit ill with the play as a whole and necessi-
tates cutting.* This could be most easily explained by a
personal emphasis, which may even be unintentional, on the
part of the author.

As long ago as 1884, J. M. Raich pointed out that Shakespeare's first, and often only, thought at the approach of
death for any of his characters 'is of God and His mercy,
of prayer, repentance, confession and the viaticum; regret
at the absence of a priest on such occasions is frequently
expressed—all this in the spirit of the Middle Ages, when
the faithful used to be instructed in a special chapter of
the catechism in the art of dying.' And if, in *Hamlet*, his
concern had not yet reached the point of *Measure for Measure*,
written three years later, in which he has no less than seven
references to the necessity of a priest at a death-bed, there
is still sufficient to be impressive.

The elder Hamlet's lament that he was

> cut off even in the blossoms of my sin,
> Unhouseled, unanointed, unannealed

(that is to say, without the Last Sacraments) is, in a sense, the
mainspring of the whole action, since it is his pitiful state in
consequence of this that makes his son determine on revenge
and at the same time prevents him accomplishing it when,
on the natural plane, it would be both safe and easy to do
so. He cannot kill Claudius at prayer, because

> He took my father grossly, full of bread,
> With all his crimes broad-blown, as flush as May
>   . . . and am I then revenged
> To take him in the purging of his soul
> When he is fit and seasoned for his passage?

Again, in the 'maimed rites' of Ophelia's funeral and the
refusal of a Requiem Mass to one whose 'death was doubtful'
the subject is again given inescapably dramatic emphasis.

* I am indebted to Mr Norman Marshall for pointing this out to me.

It should be unnecessary to point out that Ophelia's
funeral is in strict accordance with Catholic dogma and
ritual – indeed one critic has expressed astonishment at
Shakespeare's 'curiously accurate (almost recondite)' knowledge of 'mediaeval' practices – were it not that the late
Canon Percy Dearmer's extraordinary lucubrations have
been given disproportionate influence by their appearance
in the notes of Professor Dover Wilson's edition of *Hamlet*.
The 'maimed rites' are in accordance with those prescribed
by Canon Law (*Codex juris canonici*, 1240. par. 2, which
specifically deals with those whose 'death is doubtful') and a
Requiem Mass was forbidden. Burial in consecrated ground
was, as a general rule, refused. In the Anglican Church there
was no prohibition of the burial of a suicide in the churchyard till half a century after Shakespeare's death; nor did
such a thing as a Requiem Mass exist in Anglicanism.
Canon Dearmer explains 'requiem' as a 'solemn music,'
which may stand without comment.

On the other hand, Shakespeare almost certainly drew
on his memory for aspects of Ophelia's death and comments
on it. When he was sixteen – in 1580 – a girl named Katharine
Hamlett was drowned in the Avon, at a spot where the roots
of a great willow dammed the current and made a deep
pool. The inquest continued for eight weeks and was something of a *cause célèbre* in Stratford. The final verdict was
of accidental death – that the girl had slipped when leaning
over the bank – but a page of the register, which would
help to understand the suggestion of suicide, had been torn
out.

We have become so accustomed to the plot of *Hamlet*,
which, for most of us, has taken on the inevitability of an
historical circumstance, that it is difficult to imagine Shakespeare inventing and placing the scenes in his original writing
of it. But at least it is not inconsistent with probability to
suppose that the Ophelia scene, as well as the Ghost scene,
was written at Stratford in that September of John Shake-

speare's funeral, when a walk to the place of Katharine Hamlett's death would intensify the memory of the arguments about Christian burial which engaged father and son twenty-one years before.

By the end of the year, Shakespeare was once more in London, where his patron, Southampton, still lay a close prisoner in the Tower.

VI : The Earl of Southampton

IT was on April 10, 1603, less than three weeks after the death of Queen Elizabeth, that Southampton, by the express command of the new King, James of Scotland, was released from the Tower. Shakespeare celebrated the occasion in one of his best-known sonnets:

> Not mine own fears, nor the prophetic soul
> Of the wide world dreaming on things to come
> Can yet the lease of my true love control,
> Suppos'd as forfeit to a confin'd doom.
> The mortal moon hath her eclipse endur'd,
> And the sad augurs mock their own presage;
> Incertainties now crown themselves assur'd
> And peace proclaims olives of endless age.
> Now with the drops of this most balmy time
> My love looks fresh, and Death to me subscribes,
> Since, spite of him, I'll live in this poor rhyme,
> While he insults o'er dull and speechless tribes;
> And thou in this shalt find thy monument,
> When tyrants' crests and tombs of brass are spent.*

* It is not my purpose to enter here the controversy about the dating of this Sonnet which is a literary 'crux.' Its application is almost too obvious and one is again surprised at Sir Edmund Chambers, once more neglecting to tie together the literary and the historical, writing 'there can be no reference to anybody's imprisonment.' Shakespeare's fears for Southampton; the national curiosity as to what James's reign would bring; the release of the prisoner from his 'confin'd' doom; the death of Elizabeth, the 'mortal moon'; the contradiction by events of the prophecies of national disturbances consequent on the death; the

Henry Wriothesley, third Earl of Southampton, to whom the greater part of the Sonnets were addressed and both *Venus and Adonis* and *The Rape of Lucrece* dedicated, was nine and a half years younger than the poet. In 1592 when they had first become acquainted, Shakespeare was twenty-eight and Southampton, at eighteen and a half, was still 'a child of state' – a ward of the Crown. His father, the second Earl, had suffered persecution for the Faith and, at the age of thirty-six, had died in the Tower after four years imprisonment for his part in endeavouring to arrange a marriage between the Duke of Norfolk and Mary Queen of Scots. Young Henry, who was eight at the time, succeeded to the title but became a ward of the Crown and was, at Burleigh's orders, educated as a Protestant, in spite of the protests of his mother. She remained to the end of her life an open and uncompromising Catholic as befitted the daughter of that Lord Montague who had been the only member of the House of Lords brave enough to protest against the anti-Catholic legislation and who had been subsequently proceeded against because he insisted on baptising his son rather than hazard the possible invalidity of the Anglican ceremony.

Though the Dowager Countess was unable successfully to oppose the all-powerful Cecils in the matter of her son's education, she maintained a Catholic tutor named Swithin Wells, described in a Privy Council warrant of 1582 as 'a dangerous Papist.' Swithin was the real master of the young Earl and, as he was a sportsman as well as a scholar, his influence over his charge who loved the pleasures of the chase was considerable.

uncertainty of the succession now dissipated by the succession of James 'the Peacemaker' to the crown – all these are too clearly stated to make argument profitable or (in my view) possible. It is interesting to note that in his *The Original Order of Shakespeare's Sonnets*, Sir Denys Bray puts immediately preceding this one, 'If my dear love were but the child of state' (124) which gains immeasureably in depth if written by Shakespeare during Southampton's imprisonment.

Burleigh, however, introduced his spies into the Southampton household and in due course Wells and a young priest named Edward Gennings, who had said Mass in his lodgings, were for that crime hanged in front of Gray's Inn, where Southampton was studying law. To replace Wells, Burleigh appointed a Protestant dictionary-maker, Giovanni Florio, whose ostensible duty was to teach Italian and French, but whose real work was to act as informer-in-chief from his privileged position within the family circle. Florio did his work well and in his old age was able to boast of his prowess in the destruction of Papists.

Southampton's town mansion in Holborn was during most of the 'eighties and the early 'nineties well known to the authorities as one of the great Catholic centres of London. Among the recorded examinations of suspects a considerable number are noted as frequenting it or living near it. Yet, on the surface, Southampton at this time gave the appearance of conformity. As a Royal ward, as host to the Queen when she visited the town from which he took his title and as the 'somewhat wild' leader of the younger set at Court, Southampton found it almost *de rigueur*. Nor, in contemporary life, were the divisions as hard and fast as history may make them appear. To us the magnificence of the martyrs, who saved the Faith, dwarfs the memory of the lesser men who were not called on to compass that heroism. But a 'Papist' was not necessarily a recusant; a recusant was not necessarily a convicted recusant; and even a convicted and known recusant might, and on occasions did, 'go to church' to save, because it was his duty as head of a family to do so, the remnants of his inheritance. More particularly in cases of men like (in their very different social and economic spheres) Shakespeare and Southampton, whose parents' witness was unmistakable, obstinate recusancy was hardly to be expected.

At the beginning of the 'nineties, the persecution sharpened.

A Royal Proclamation against Catholics in the October of 1591, followed by a new Act against them in 1593, coincides with the publication of Shakespeare's first work, *Venus and Adonis*, dedicated to Southampton, and with his attaching himself to Holborn House. Among the victims of the persecution was another poet, Robert Southwell, a distant cousin of Shakespeare and, by marriage, twice 'cousin' to Southampton.*

Robert Southwell, born in Norfolk in 1561 – and thus three years older than Shakespeare – had been brought up a Catholic, sent abroad, and educated at Douai. At the age of seventeen, he was admitted to the Society of Jesus in Rome (where he knew Simon Hunt, Shakespeare's Stratford schoolmaster, who was also with him at Douai) and was ordained priest in 1584, the same year as Robert Debdale, who was hanged, drawn and quartered at Tyburn in the October of 1586, three months after Southwell himself arrived on 'the English Mission' with Father Henry Garnet. For six years he ministered to Catholics in England, living as a country gentleman, visiting the great Catholic houses under various disguises and the prisons where Catholics lay. It was an apostolate which in many ways recalled that of Blessed Edmund Campion, his forerunner in martyrdom.

But he was also a poet, one of the most popular of the day, who put his genius at the service of his religion and used the idiom of the time – even Euphuism – to teach the truths of the Faith. The licensing of this work and its open sale – there were ten editions of his poems in his short lifetime – were in all probability due to the patronage of Southampton.

* Southwell's brother and sister had each married Southampton's first cousins. Southwell's relationship to Shakespeare is through the Vaux and the Throckmortons. Genealogical tables illustrating both connections appear in *The Life of Robert Southwell* by Christopher Devlin (1956) which contains in full the argument – there for the first time printed – for Southwell's influence on Shakespeare which I am here assuming to be correct.

In 1592 Southwell was betrayed and captured and atrociously tortured thirteen times to try to make him reveal the names and whereabouts of secret Catholics. His steadfastness impressed even Robert Cecil, who admitted to a friend: 'They boast about the heroes of antiquity . . . but we have a new torture which it is not possible for a man to bear. And yet I have seen Robert Southwell hanging by it, still as a tree trunk, and no one able to drag one word from his mouth.'

A few months before his arrest in the June of 1592 Southwell collected all his poems into book-form in the order he wished them to be published. He divided them into three parts, each with its own dedication. Shakespeare's *Venus and Adonis*, with its dedication to Southampton, was already in manuscript. Southwell's dedication of the second part of his poems was also to Southampton, urging him to encourage those he patronised to turn to Christian themes, as he himself had done:

> This makes my mourning Muse resolve in tears,
>   This makes my heavy pen to 'plain in prose:
> Christ's thorn is sharp, no head his garland wears,
>   Still finest wits are stilling Venus's rose:
>   In Paynim toys the sweetest veins are spent,
>   To Christian works few have their talents lent.
>
> License my single pen to seek a phere;
>   You heavenly sparks of wit show native light;
> Cloud not with misty loves your orient clear;
>   Sweet flights you shoot, learn once to level right.
>   Favour my wish; well-wishing works no ill;
>   I move the suit, the grant rests in your will.

The dedication of the third part of Southwell's poems was 'to my worthy good cousin, Master W. S.,' but until 1616, the year of Shakespeare's death, the printed copies abbreviated it to: 'The author to his loving cousin.' In this dedication, which is in prose, he returned to the same theme as the second, urging poets to cherish their talents and use them to good ends. He had already, in his preface to his *Mary Magdalen's Funeral Tears*, published in 1591, written: 'In fables are often figured moral truths and that covertly uttered to a common good which, without mask, would not find so free a passage,' so there was no question of the 'Christian poem' being overt.

In 1593 Shakespeare wrote and in 1594 published the 'graver labour' *The Rape of Lucrece*, which he had promised Southampton in his dedication to *Venus and Adonis*. This time his tone, under the decorous prose of the dedication, takes on something of the love expressed in the Sonnets: 'What I have done is yours; what I have to do is yours; being part in all I have, devoted yours.' And the atmosphere of *Lucrece* is so very different from that of *Venus and Adonis* that it is not impossible to suppose, even were there no other evidence, that Southampton had rightly read Southwell's dedication: 'I move the suit; the grant rests in your Will,' and that Shakespeare, moved by Southwell's dedication to him, had tried to use his talent to a worthier end and, under the form of a 'fable,' had written of the violation of a soul by sin. For this is the real 'allegory' of *Lucrece*, which, as Hales pointed out over seventy years ago in his preface to Ward's *English Poets*, 'remind one curiously of the almost exactly contemporary poem,' Southwell's *Peter's Plaint*. Despite their very different subject matter, both poems are concerned with 'the anatomy of sin.'

Southwell, for example, writes:

> This fawning viper, dumb till he has wounded
> With many mouths, doth now upbraid my harms;
> My sight was veiled till I myself confounded,
> Then did I see the disenchanted charms.

Shakespeare, more dramatic, parallels this with:

> O deeper sin that bottomless conceit

Can comprehend in still imagination!
Drunken desire must vomit his receipt
Ere he can see his own abomination . . .

A careful analysis of the two poems yields surprising results for, as Christopher Devlin has pointed out, even in their use of conceits and images they both drew not from contemporary fashion but from the humanism of the Fathers.

That Shakespeare knew, admired and was influenced by Southwell's poetry is admitted by all literary critics. That Shakespeare knew Southwell himself is not less certain since, quite apart from their kinship, their common friends and their common patron, their frequenting of Holborn House would make meeting, in the circumstances of time, inevitable. All else is in the realm of probability; yet the circumstantial evidence is strong that Southwell's last dedication was to Shakespeare as an earnest of his belief that the younger but greater poet would use his genius 'for the greater glory of God.'

Hardly had *Lucrece* appeared than, in the same year, a libel entitled '*Willobie his Avisa* or the true picture of a modest maid and a chaste and constant wife' was published with an Oxford imprint. In essence it was an attack on the wife of an Oxford innkeeper, easily identifiable as John Davenant who kept the Golden Crown Inn in Oxford. The piece was a parody of *Lucrece*. It pointed out that the perfect spouse is a rare bird (rara Avis or Avisa) – 'Let Lucres – Avis be thy name' – and left no doubt that under the exterior of a Lucrece could be found a wanton. Mrs Davenant, 'a very beautiful woman and of a very good wit and of conversation extremely agreeable,' is better known in history as 'the Dark Lady of the Sonnets'* and the object of a temporary rivalry between Shakespeare and Southampton who were together in Oxford in the autumn of 1592. The pseudonymous author makes the situation plain enough. 'W.S.,' an actor, advises

* *See footnote on page 60.*

his friend, the noble 'Harry W.' (ostensibly 'Henry
Willoughby' but clearly enough Southampton) on the
subject of the enthralling charms of the much-wooed Avisa,
from which he has also suffered much, in terms

> She is no saint, she is no nun!
> I think in time she may be won

recalling a couplet which, in one form or another, Shakespeare had introduced into no less than three of his early
plays. To emphasise the identity of Southampton, 'Harry W.'
continually quotes proverbs from the collection just brought
out by Florio, who was with him on the Oxford visit.†

The censor speedily suppressed the libel, nor is the work of
any value except in so far as it gives the background for the

* It is unfortunate that the name of Mary Fitton (who was fair) has
been given currency as 'the Dark Lady' by various popular romances,
including plays by Bernard Shaw, Frank Harris and Clemence Dane.
There is no reason to suppose that Mary Fitton, a Maid of Honour at
Court, ever knew Shakespeare and she only appears in the story because
in 1890 Thomas Tyler, rejecting the traditional – and, from the historical
point of view, inevitable – identification of the beloved friend and patron
as Southampton, advanced the claims of the Earl of Pembroke, who
had an intrigue with Mary Fitton in 1601. The inconsistencies of this
identification, though dear to the romantic' Nineties, are akin to Baconian
cyphers. They involve the rejection of simple and accepted hypotheses
in favour of strained interpretations which have no historical background.

The *Sonnets* are dedicated by the publisher, Thorpe, to Southampton's
stepfather, William Harvey, the third husband of the Dowager Countess.
When she died, in 1607, she left him her sole legatee and he was responsible, according to the dedication, for granting and procuring authori-
sation to publish the MS in 1609. William Harvey had earlier appeared
as 'W.H.' in another dedication in 1606 – the dedication of Robert
Southwell's *Fourfold Meditation*.

Tyler interpreted 'Mr W.H.' as being William Herbert, Earl of
Pembroke; and, once the initials were supposed to be those of the poet's
object of affection instead of the publisher's object of gratitude, the way
was opened for every vagary of speculation, from Oscar Wilde's 'Willy
Hughes,' a non-existent boy-actor, to 'William Himself.'

The case for Southampton does not at all rest on the coincidence
that Henry Wriothesley 'gives the same initials in reverse, but on the
historical relationship of the *Sonnets* to the known life of Shakespeare's
patron and friend.

great series of Sonnets in which Shakespeare revealed the inwardness of it —

> Two loves I have of comfort and despair,
>   Which like two spirits do suggest me still:
> The better angel is a man right fair,
>   The worser spirit a woman colour'd ill . . .

and

> That thou hast her, it is not all my grief
>   And yet it may be said I lov'd her dearly:
> That she hath thee is of my wailing chief,
>   A loss in love that toucheth me more nearly . . .

and

> So, now I have confess'd that he is thine,
>   And I myself am mortgag'd to thy will,
> Myself I'll forfeit, so that other mine
>   Thou wilt restore to be my comfort still . . .

and indeed all those poems which have always been seen as 'the drama of the sonnets,' the key with which Shakespeare unlocked his heart.

Shakespeare himself did not escape the 'Dark Lady's' spell. On his visits to Oxford he stayed with the Davenants and became godfather to their son, William, for whom he had a special affection. That the boy was in fact his son there seems no reason to doubt. The story is of contemporary origin and Davenant always assumed the paternity. The boy's brother remembered Shakespeare giving him 'a hundred kisses.' One of the Oxford dons, noticing young Davenant rushing home from school, asked him where he was going in such a hurry, to be told: 'Oh, sir, my godfather is come to town and I am going to ask his blessing.' The learned Doctor replied: 'Hold, child. You should not take the name of God in vain.' Later, when Davenant himself became a poet and playwright (he was made Poet Laureate

† *Willobie his Avisa* raises other problems and has other bearings than this particular one; but they are not relevant to this essay.

at the age of thirty-two) a satirical attack on him discovered
'Avon' as a component of his name – 'D'Avenant from Avon
comes.'

Of Shakespeare's continuing relationship with Southampton there is no firm 'documentary evidence' such as academic
historians insist on. There is no reason why there should be;
but an understanding of human nature might suggest
that it is unnecessary to postulate on that account a cessation
of friendship, however their different worlds might appear
to sunder them. The Countess de Chambrun has an illuminat-
ing passage on the reflection of Southampton's interests in
Shakespeare's plays: 'Should Henry Wriothesley bury
himself in the study of law, the language of the poet is filled
with legal terms. Is he dreaming of serving the King of
France? Shakespeare's comedies transport the spectator
to Nerac or the Louvre. When his taste turns to the stories
of Cinthio and Boccaccio, Shakespeare finds new inspiration
from Italian subjects taken from the *Novelle*. When Mon-
taigne's Essays appeared in England, translated by Florio,
Shakespeare was the first to rally to the new fashion and
utilise the writings of the French humanist . . . and, later,
when his patron threw himself into the great colonial
enterprise of the Virginia Company and became its secretary,
equipping ships to link the mother country to the young
colonies, it was the wreck of the barque *Sea Adventure* on
the Bermudan shore which provided the subject of *The
Tempest* . . .

'Moreover, if Shakespeare's work permits us to appreciate
Southampton, in his turn Southampton often helps the
understanding of Shakespeare's texts. The life of this great
nobleman throws light on certain passages which appear
obscure. In the hundred and fifth Sonnet, for example, when
the poet declares that his songs and praises are dedicated 'to
one, of one, still such, and ever so,' the puzzled commentators
have thought there is a misprint. However, the phrase
alludes to the heraldic device of Henry Wriothesley:

'Ung partout, tout par ung' and the sonnet is thus a variation on the theme of the Southampton coat of arms.'

Southampton survived Shakespeare by only eight years. Some time before his death and within seven years of Shakespeare's, a monument to the poet was erected in Stratford Church and someone (it is not known who) sent the epitaph which is now engraved there:

Judicio Pylium, Genio Socratem, Arte Maronem
Terra tegit, populus maeret, Olympus habet.

Stay passenger, why goest thou by so fast?
Read, if thou canst, whom envious Death hath plast
Within this monument, Shakespeare, with whome
Quick Nature dide; whose name doth decke ys tombe
Far more than cost, sith all yt he hath writt
Leaves living art, but page, to serve his witt
　　　　Obiit Ano dni 1616 Aetatis 53. Die 23. Ap.

Of all the suggestions of the possible writer, the most likely is the hypothesis of Dr Carmichael Stopes that it was Southampton.* She points out that, on the evidence of the Sonnets – 71, 72 and 81 in particular – they had discussed their deaths. Sonnet 81 runs:

Or I shall live your epitaph to make,
Or you survive when I in earth am rotten,
From hence your memory death cannot take,
Although in me each part will be forgotten.
Your name from hence immortal life shall have,
Though I, once gone, to all the world must die;
The earth can yield me but a common grave,
When you entombed in all men's eyes shall lie.
Your monument shall be my gentle verse,
Which eyes not yet created shall o'er-read:

* See pp 381–383 of *The Third Earl of Southampton* (CUP 1922).

And tongues to be your being shall rehearse.
When all the breathers of this world are dead,
  You still shall live – such virtue hath my pen –
  Where breath most breathes, even in the mouths of
    men.

And in Sonnet 72 Shakespeare issues the half-challenge:

O, lest the world should task you to recite
What merit lived in me, that you should love
After my death, dear love, forget me quite,
For you in me can nothing worthy prove;
Unless you would devise some virtuous lie,
To do more for me than mine own desert
And hang more praise upon deceased I
Than niggard truth would willingly impart . . .

Is it not probable that Southampton took up the challenge and in 'Shakespeare with whom quick Nature died' devised the 'virtuous lie' which was truer than 'niggard truth?'

This is no more than a guess; yet it is one which takes account of the probabilities and realities of the time and which treats Shakespeare and Southampton as living people instead of as terms of an academic cryptogram. Dr Stopes says of the theory: 'I only wish to suggest that it is possible, and not even improbable, that the "Lord of his love" may have added a survivor's memorial on the cold stone.'

And there is one supporting argument for it which Dr Stopes overlooked and which classical pedantry unwittingly supports. Summing up opinions on it, Sir Edmund Chambers wrote: 'It was no very accurate scholar who shortened the first vowel of "Socratem." Steevens conjectured "Sopho-clem." ' It might seem indeed that Sophocles, as dramatist, was more appropriate, especially in conjunction with the poet Virgil. But would not the one person who would insist on the analogy of Shakespeare to Socrates be his Alcibiades?

The relationship of Shakespeare and Southampton, as portrayed in the Sonnets, has been and will continue to be the subject of argument, oscillating between Hallam's: 'There is a weakness and folly in all misplaced affection which is not redeemed by the touches of nobler sentiments that abound in this long series of sonnets. It is impossible not to wish that Shakespeare had never written them' to the judgment of their latest (and, in many ways, most perceptive) interpreter, J. B. Leishman, that there is 'no real precedent in previous love-poetry either for Shakespeare's topic or for Shakespeare's treatment of it' and that the Sonnets are 'the most wonderful expression of "possessionless love" in all literature.'*

Moreover, approaching them from a very different angle from this essay and (although almost alone among commentators dating the 'Mortal moon' sonnet correctly) inclining to the belief that Pembroke rather than Southampton was the beloved youth,† Mr Leishman sees in them 'that almost religious adoration of a person which would have been

* *Themes and Variations in Shakespeare's Sonnets* (1961).

† William Herbert, third Earl of Pembroke was sixteen years younger than Shakespeare and did not come to London till 1598 by which time Shakespeare had written the three parts of *Henry VI*, *Richard III*, *The Comedy of Errors*, *Titus Andronicus*, *Two Gentlemen of Verona*, *Love's Labour's Lost*, *Romeo and Juliet*, *Richard II*, *A Midsummer Night's Dream*, *King John*, *The Merchant of Venice* and the two parts of *Henry IV* – and been in trouble over Falstaff. It thus seems unlikely that he would, in the first group of sonnets urging the youth to marry, refer to 'my pupil pen.' Also the line 'You had a father: let your son say so' suggests that the youth's father was dead – as Southampton's, of course, was: Pembroke's did not die till 1601. Even the 'Pembrokians' theory that the 'marriage' sonnets refer to William Herbert's father's attempt to betroth him, aged 15, to Sir George Carey's daughter in 1595 is subject to the objection that the matter occupied only two months and that it came to nothing, not because the boy objected, but because Carey refused to pay £1,000 a year dowry. On the other hand, all the necessary conditions are fulfilled if the 'marriage-sonnets' are written to Southampton in 1590 – two years before *Venus and Adonis* – when, as we know from the correspondence between Southampton's mother, Burleigh, Montague and Sir Thomas Stanhope (see *The Third Earl of Southampton*, pp. 36–39) pressure was being put on the seventeen-year-old Southampton to marry Elizabeth Vere.

Supporting the claim of Pembroke as the youth, Sir Edmund Chambers writes: 'It is a striking fact that, although Southampton was impossible before the advent of Christianity' and, in a masterly analysis, is concerned with 'the "religiousness" of so many of Shakespeare's expressions of his love.'

'Even apart from Shakespeare's characteristic manner of expression,' he writes, 'I can find nothing in other love-poetry really comparable with his many variations on the theme of what I have called "compensation" and I think the only things in other poetry of which they really "remind" me are some of those poems where George Herbert expresses or, as it were, revivifies his conviction that his "pearl of great price" is more than sufficient compensation for all that either he himself or the world may have supposed him to have resigned or foregone; perhaps, too, certain things in Henry Vaughan.' And again: 'In sonnet after sonnet and in one universalising and, as it were, annihilating metaphor after another Shakespeare has conveyed the impression that there is nothing either in this world or above it that can compare with the meaningfulness to him of his friend . . . and one can never feel quite certain, and perhaps Shakespeare himself could never feel quite certain, whether what he is celebrating is the beloved or the love which the beloved has inspired.'

This might be interpreted strictly – as Mr Leishman has noticed – as idolatry. But Shakespeare was aware of that danger:

> Let not my love be called idolatry,
> Nor my beloved as an idol show.

Nor is there any reason to suppose that the intense perception and love of the truth, beauty and charity of the human lover:

still alive, it was not to him but to Herbert and his brother that the Folio was dedicated.' If Shakespeare himself had dedicated the Folio to Pembroke alone, the fact might be 'striking'; but Shakespeare had been dead seven years before it appeared in 1623 and, in consequence, had nothing to do with the actor-editors' diplomatic dedication to Pembroke, who was Lord Chamberlain at the time, and his brother and heir who succeeded him in the office.

> 'Fair, kind and true' is all my argument,
>   'Fair, kind and true' varying to other words:
> And in this change is my invention spent,
> Three themes in one which wondrous scope afford.
>   'Fair, kind and true' have often lived alone,
>   Which three till now never kept seat in one –

should not lead him, as it has classically led others, to the love of the Holy Trinity.

Shakespeare's love for Southampton was platonic in both senses of that much misused word. It was the love of a man for a man – Plato's 'Heavenly Love,' passing the love of women – and it was sexually unindulged. It was 'a marriage of true minds,' but it was not a gratified lust. About this there cannot really be any argument. Shakespeare himself stated it as categorically as it has ever been stated in the very sonnet which has been too casually accepted as evidence of his 'homosexuality':

> A woman's face with Nature's own hand painted
> Hast thou, the master-mistress of my passion

With a physiological pun, he insists:

> And for a woman wert thou first created;
>   Till Nature, as she wrought thee, fell a-doting,
> And by addition me of thee defeated,
>   By adding one thing to my purpose nothing
>   But since she prick'd thee out for women's
>   pleasure,
>   Mine be thy love, and thy love's use their
>   treasure.

That Southampton did not return Shakespeare's love with any approach to equivalence is evident from the sonnets themselves and inferent from the temporal circumstances which made the one a great nobleman and the other a poor player. To quote Mr Leishman again, 'nowhere, one might almost say, in Shakespeare's sonnets, is there unmistakable evidence that Shakespeare really believed that his friend, in any deep and meaningful sense of the word, loved him at all. At most, perhaps, his friend "quite liked him." Saddest of all, I think, are those sonnets where Shakespeare speaks of their difference in rank, and sometimes of his own profession, as an insuperable barrier between them.'

It is indeed ironical that in those poems in which Shakespeare (in George Saintsbury's words) 'caught up the sum of love and uttered it as no poet has before or since and . . . carried poetry to a pitch which it had never previously reached in English and which it has never outstepped since' to immortalise Southampton, he also inevitably, if unintentionally, left on record for ever Southampton's unworthiness of that love. Nowhere in literature has there been such support of Plato's paradoxical perception that 'the god is in the lover, not in the beloved.' And nowhere in the sonnets themselves is there a greater expression of 'possessionless love' which saints and artists have known as one of the ways to God* than that poem which was surely written in 1601, when Southampton was in prison:

> Tired with all these, for restful death I cry:
>   As, to behold desert a beggar born,
> And needy nothing trimm'd in jollity,
>   And purest faith unhappily forsworn,
> And gilded honour shamefully misplac'd,
>   And maiden honour rudely strumpeted,
> And right perfection wrongfully disgrac'd,
>   And strength by limping sway disabled,
> And art made tongue-tied by authority,
>   And folly, doctor-like, controlling skill,
> And simple truth miscall'd simplicity,
>   And captive good attending captain ill.
>   Tired with all these, from these I would be gone,
>   Save that, to die, I leave my love alone.

* For a further examination of this point, see the chapter 'The Nature of Love' in *The Arrow and the Sword* (1947).

VII: *Measure for Measure*

WITH the accession of James I, son of Mary Queen of Scots who had died for the Faith, the Catholics of England entertained some hope of the toleration he had secretly promised them. And, indeed, for the first nine months of the reign there was some evidence that he intended to keep his word. In the July of 1603, he received a Catholic deputation, whose spokesman was Sir Thomas Tresham (brother-in-law of the Edward Arden who was executed in the Somerville affair), and promised to remit the recusancy fines. In August he learnt, through the Papal Nuncios in Paris and Brussels, that the Pope, on his part, would countenance no insurrection of Catholics and that any Catholics conspiring against the State would incur ecclesiastical censures, and for the remainder of the year the atmosphere was so peaceful that no less than a hundred and forty priests entered England, the chapels of the Catholic embassies were thrown open and 'in some sections sermons were delivered in the open air to which the faithful flocked by thousands.'

Nevertheless the change was less promising than it appeared, for Cecil, the architect of persecution, was still the ruler of England, even though it was not till he had availed himself of the 'Gunpowder Plot' of 1605 to terrorise the King into enthusiastic anti-Catholicism that he controlled James as firmly as he had controlled Elizabeth since the Essex rebellion. He told the Venetian Ambassador, however, with unequivocal directness: 'There are laws

and they must be observed and there is no doubt but that
the object of these laws is to extinguish the Catholic religion
in this kingdom' and in the February of 1604 the King was
induced to issue an order for all Catholic priests to leave
the country – the proclamation was made on Ash Wednesday – though at the opening of Parliament in March James
made it clear that he considered this a political move only
and that he had no intention of persecuting the Catholic
laity or of enforcing the recusancy fines. The Venetian
Ambassador, in his dispatch to the Doge, observed that
'the tone of his speech showed a disposition very favourable
to the Catholics and it is a fact that, in spite of the proclamation, very few priests have left the Kingdom and no great
diligence is used towards their expulsion; even those who are
actually in prison and could easily be expelled have not
been moved yet; and the Catholics begin to entertain lively
hopes.'

The slowness in restarting the persecution after the re-
enactment of the Elizabethan laws was due in part to the
fact that in the summer the Constable of Castile was to visit
England to conclude peace with Spain and that it was
possible that the treatment of English Catholics would
come under discussion. At the moment, the Constable
was in Brussels, conducting the necessary negotiations,
and to him Thomas Winter travelled, as the spokesman of
the Catesby 'cousinage,' to 'entreat him to solicit His
Majesty at his coming hither that the penal laws may be
recalled and we admitted into the rank of his other subjects.'
Winter saw the Constable, delivered his message 'in the
name of all the Catholics of England' and was assured by the
Constable that 'he had strict command from His Majesty
of Spain to do all good offices for the Catholics; and, for
his own part, he thought himself bound in conscience so to
do and that no good occasion should be omitted.' But in
spite of fair promises, Winter was convinced that nothing
would be done 'Good words,' as he told Catesby on his

return in April, 'but I fear the deeds will not answer.' Spain's political need for peace was too great to allow consideration for English Catholics to constitute an obstacle to it.

In England, Cecil and his fellow-millionaires were determined that, whatever the King's private inclinations, the balance of property was not going to be altered* and during the summer assizes of 1604, on the eve of the Constable's visit, the judges on circuit ignored the King's expressed wishes and returned to Elizabethan punishments. At Warwick, on July 16, another example was made. Fr John Sugar was hanged, drawn and quartered for saying Mass, and Robert Grissold, a gentleman of Rowington, nine miles from Stratford-on-Avon, was hanged for sheltering priests.

The Constable of Castile arrived in London on August 10 and left on August 26. During that time, he and his suite were lodged in Somerset House, were entertained with some magnificence and 'attended by the Gentlemen Ushers, sewers, cooks, Yeomen of the Guard and Grooms of the Chamber.' But these did not yield sufficient servants for the occasion and, the account adds, 'the King's Players, being Grooms of the Chamber Extraordinary, are summoned for that purpose.' So Shakespeare too – for his company was now known as the King's Players – waited on the Constable, but in a very different capacity from his cousin, Thomas Winter. For a fortnight he, with eleven other actors, served, in their red liveries, at Somerset House. It was a public

* From the beginning of the 'Reformation' to the last act of it in the 'Glorious Revolution' of 1688, the redistribution of property is the key to anti-Catholicism. As the great Protestant historian, R. H. Tawney, has put it, the Reformation was a revolution which ensured 'a sweeping redistribution of wealth, carried out by an unscrupulous minority, using the weapons of violence, intimidation and fraud, and succeeded by an orgy of interested misgovernment on the part of its principal beneficiaries.' The abiding fear of the new owners, represented in Elizabethan and Jacobean times by the ruling Cecils, was that, if Catholicism were re-established, an Abbey might become an abbey again instead of the favourite country residence of a Protestant millionaire.

reminder of the status he had bewailed in his sonnets to
Southampton, who himself was, by reason of his rank, the
chief attendant on the Constable and who, at one of the
banquets 'led out the Queen and three other gentlemen
their several partners, who all joined in dancing a brando.'

It is tempting to think – and at least as probable as any
other hypothesis that has been advanced – that it was at this
time that Shakespeare wrote to Southampton:

> Let me confess that we two must be twain
> Although our undivided loves are one;
> So shall these blots that do with me remain,
> Without they help by me be borne alone.
> In our two loves there is but one respect,
> Though in our lives a separable spite,
> Which though it alter not love's sole effect,
> Yet it doth steal sweet hours from love's delight.
> I may not evermore acknowledge thee,
> Lest my bewailed guilt* should do thee shame,
> Nor thou with public kindness honour me,
> Unless thou take that honour from thy name
>   But do not so; I love thee in such sort
>   As thou being mine, mine is thy good report.

As Thomas Winter had foreseen, no good, in the matter of
toleration of Catholics, came from the Constable's visit.
At Manchester the judges, after condemning many to death
including a layman who had merely 'entertained a Jesuit,'
laid it down that, as the law stood, anyone who heard Mass
thereby incurred the death penalty. An aged Lancashire man,
Thomas Pound, who had suffered long imprisonment for
the Faith under Elizabeth, determined to test the truth of
this statement and presented to the King a humble petition,

---

* That this is a punning reference to his livery is the more possible
since in the following year he used a similar one in *Macbeth* where Lady
Macbeth, taking back two blood-stained daggers to Duncan's chamber,
says: 'I'll gild the faces of the grooms withal, for it must seem their guilt.'

calling attention to the renewal of persecution and to the
Manchester ruling. He asked that an independent commission should be appointed to inquire into the proceedings
of the assize judges. The Privy Council immediately ordered
him to be arrested. He was brought before the Star Chamber
where he was abused and browbeaten, told by Cecil that he
was 'a weak and feeble-witted old man,' sententiously
addressed by the Archbishop of Canterbury who quoted
St Cyprian at him ('which Mr Pound peremptorily reproved
saying it was St Jerome and not St Cyprian, whereto the
Archbishop replied not') and sentenced to be imprisoned
during the King's pleasure, to pay a fine of £1,000 and to
stand in the pillory at Lancaster and at Westminster. A
majority of the Privy Council, including Cecil's brother,
Burghley, pressed for the additional punishment that he
should be nailed to the pillory and have both his ears cut off,
one in London, one in Lancaster, but this was eventually
overruled, though Cecil insisted that, while he stood in the
pillory, placards stating his crime should be hung on him
and the Archbishop of Canterbury laid down the general
principle, in a diatribe against Rome as 'the purple harlot
and the seat of Anti-Christ', that as Catholics refused to
inform against each other, it was necessary 'to put some
Judas among them.'

Later in the autumn – in the November – the King
ordered a new Anglican translation of the Bible (the
'Authorised Version') and prepared to entertain his Danish
brother-in-law, Ulric, who was duly lodged at Court and
allowed twenty dishes of meat at every meal. As, on November
30, it was announced 'there is a new copy of *The Tragical
History of Hamlet, Prince of Denmark* imprinted, and enlarged
to almost as much again as it was in the former, according
to the true and perfect copy' it may be assumed that first-
hand acquaintance with Danish nobility and their habits
supplied Shakespeare with some matter for the 'enlargement' and that the printing of what is now known as the

First Quarto had an air of topicality, even if it had no longer the tragic compactness of the play he had written in 1601.

Whether or not Shakespeare had written *Othello* before James's accession there is no means of knowing; but it was the first play of his to be performed at Court in the new reign (on November 1st). The second was *Measure for Measure* which he wrote as the Christmas play and which was performed in the Banqueting Hall on December 26. As an actor Shakespeare appeared in the small part of Friar Peter; but as an author, as Professor Chambers has pointed out, never does he 'seem more passionately to identify himself with any of his characters than he does with Isabella as she pleads for mercy against strict justice.' More than for most plays does the background of the time of writing need to be understood if the play itself is to be understood.

'I believe that *Piers Plowman* and *Measure for Measure* are the two things most widely misunderstood in English Literature, with the one exception of the works of Jonathan Swift,' wrote Professor Chambers in his preface to the volume* which contains his British Academy lecture on *Measure for Measure* which first restored intelligent criticism to the play. According to Professor Dover Wilson, Shakespeare at that time 'quite obviously believed in nothing'; according to Sir Edmund Chambers he had 'the temper of an inquisitor: you can but shudder'; Coleridge found the play 'the most painful – nay, rather, the only painful – part' of Shakespeare's works; Swinburne considered that the audience is 'lured and led on to look for some equitable and satisfying upshot, defrauded and derided and sent empty away'; Hazlitt described Angelo as one 'whom we hate'; Quiller-Couch said that 'Isabella writes no lesson on the dark walls'; Dover Wilson that her chastity is 'rancid'; and Miss Ellis Fermor that her inhumanity is pitiless and

* *Man's Unconquerable Mind* (1939).

her virtue self-indulgent, unimaginative and self-absorbed.
Well may Professor Chambers write of 'the extraordinary
prejudice which critics cherish against all the people in
the play. 'They christen it a 'dark comedy' and then darken
the characters to justify their classification,' he writes and
makes his protest against 'the modern habit of keeping
Shakespeare's text but putting upon it a construction which
is post-Ibsen and post-Shaw; imposing an outlook and a
morality not Shakespeare's.'

It is perhaps difficult for an age which regards fornication
as an amusing inevitability, laws enforcing public morality
as an intolerable interference with individual liberty and a
belief in the Last Judgement as an atavistic opium-dream
to understand the dilemma of Isabella who can save her
brother from death for breaking the law against fornication
by committing fornication with the magistrate who can
acquit him. Indeed, to the non-Christian it cannot really
appear a dilemma at all, and even many non-Catholic
Christians – as, for instance, the late Miss Ellis Fermor –
find it difficult to forgive Isabella for her refusal.

For *Measure for Measure* is not only a Christian play. It is,
in the strictest sense of the term, a Catholic play, based as
firmly on traditional theology as a mediaeval morality.
Professor Chambers sees that 'since the Duke controls the
whole action of the play, we must see him as Shakespeare
meant us to do, or misunderstand the play.' And the role
of the Duke has been best described by M. D. H. Parker:* 'It
[the play] is a *commedia* staged not in Heaven but on earth,
where the plot is as entirely in the hands of the Duke of
Vienna as the plot of Dante's and Aquinas's universe is in
the hands of God. Of everything that happens in it, except
of "the evil of fault," his "grace like power divine" is the
cause. Yet though to this Duke God has lent not only his
office but in discernible outline his nature, the play is not

* *The Slave of Life: A Study of Shakespeare and the Idea of Justice*
(1955).

in any simple sense of the word an allegory. It is throughout
a *double entendre*, in which the metaphysical and allegorical
meaning alternates with the ethical and the personal, which
is, after all, the more explicit.'

Friar Peter describes the Duke as 'a man divine and holy';
Escalus, the 'chorus' of the play, sees him as 'one that, above
all other strifes, contented especially to know himself:
rather rejoicing to see another merry than merry at anything
which professed to make him rejoice: a gentleman of all
temperance'; Isabella, in her worst moment, remembers him
as 'the good Duke'; to Mariana he is 'a man of comfort,
whose advice Hath often still'd my brawling discontent,'
while the Duke himself describes his office:

> He who the sword of heaven will bear
> Should be as holy as severe;
> Pattern in himself to know,
> Grace to stand and virtue go;
> More nor less to others paying
> Than by self-offences weighing.

– in an address, alone on the stage and direct to an audience
grouped round the King James whose known political tenet
was the Divine Right of Kings.

The Duke, who is described by one critic as 'a power
rather than a character,' was entirely Shakespeare's invention and is not to be found in the older play, Whetstone's
Promos and Cassandra, which is generally regarded as his
source, or in Cinthio's story which is the basis for both.
The significance of this is heightened by Shakespeare
making the Duke, while supposedly absent from Vienna,
adopt the disguise of a Franciscan friar from which to watch
and control his deputy, Angelo.

'The dealings of the Duke with Angelo,' says Miss Parker,
'are in astonishing detail like the dealings of Christian
Providence with men. He is apparently absent, yet present;
he leaves with Angelo "mortality and mercy in Vienna"

to "live in thy tongue and heart," and he works up to the
last scene entirely by suggestions to others.'

In the same way, Shakespeare alters the character of the
original Cassandra to the Isabella of *Measure for Measure*
by making her a novice of the Order of St Clare, an order
'founded on a devotion at once practical and contemplative,
to the sufferings of Christ' – that Atonement for the sins
of the whole world of which she in vain reminds Angelo
is 'the remedy.' The character of the other friars, the meaning
of the Order, the continual references to confession and other
Catholic practices are all evidences of Shakespeare's intention in that year 1604 in England. And he expressed it in
hitherto unparalleled theatrical language. 'It is admitted,'
as Professor Chambers says, 'that no greater or more moving
scenes had appeared on any stage since the masterpieces
of Attic drama ceased to be acted.' These particular scenes,
involving Isabella and her brother who is condemned to
die; Angelo, the good-seeming deputy, who names his price
for mercy; and the Duke, disguised as Friar Lodowick,
involve the questions of Catholic morality and justice
arising from Isabella's refusal – which is a crucial alteration
of the old play where Cassandra consents to save her brother's
life.

Isabella is not afraid of death. She tells Claudio:

> O, were it but my life
> I'd throw it down for your deliverance
> As frankly as a pin.

But she is afraid of sin and judgment:

> Better it were a brother died at once
> Than that a sister, by redeeming him
> Should die for ever.

This is the stumbling-stone for the majority of critics and
most modern audiences, who, lacking Catholic theology, see

in this merely a fantastical excuse, just as they see in Hamlet's refusal to kill Claudius while at prayer nothing but an example of his 'procrastination.'* Shakespeare by making Isabella a nun, sworn to chastity, has made the reality as clear as possible, since, in yielding to Angelo she would be not only committing sin but breaking a most sacred vow. He is also careful to make her a novice, who has not taken the final vows, so that the Duke's offer of marriage at the close of the play may not seem too incongruous, and he has been equally careful not to let her accept it – a point often obscured in performance when the producer supplies the actress with expressions and gestures for which there is no warrant in the text. Indeed, it is impossible to think of Isabella as eventually marrying the Duke. She remains, in the words of the frivolous Lucio, 'a thing ensky'd and sainted,'

> an immortal spirit;
> And to be talked with in sincerity,
> As with a saint.

The only 'marriage' between her and the Duke is in their allegorical aspects – the marriage of justice and mercy, for which the whole play is a plea.

Once it is understood that Isabella means what she says when she tells Claudio that she is willing to die for him and explains to Angelo:

> The impression of keen whips I'd wear as rubies,
> And strip myself to death, as to a bed
> That, longing, have been sick for, ere I'd yield
> My body up to shame,

* There is, of course, no 'delay' in *Hamlet*. As soon as he is convinced that the Ghost is indeed his father and has made the final test of the play-scene, Hamlet kills Claudius (who is never without his guards) at the first opportunity. The Oedipus-complex school of critics – almost an accepted orthodoxy – who insist that Hamlet can only kill Claudius after Gertrude is dead are interesting only in so far as they exhibit their own minds.

even her much-criticised outburst when Claudio, suddenly
afraid of death, cries:

> Sweet sister, let me live;
> What sin you do to save a brother's life,
> Nature dispenses with the deed so far
> That it becomes a virtue,

becomes intelligible. This, for her, is the last, keenest and
most savage temptation. It can be met only by a kind of
unearthly vehemence. 'The fierceness of Isabel's words is
the measure of the agony of her soul. "The fortress which
parleys, the woman who parleys is lost." '

R. W. Chambers uses the analogy of the fortress to make
clearer to modernity the point of issue. She 'can no more be
expected to sell herself into mortal sin than a good soldier
can be expected to sell a stronghold entrusted to him.
Imagine an officer and his subaltern commanded to hold
to the uttermost a fortified post against rebels. In a sortie the
rebels capture the subaltern, and threaten to shoot him
unless the fort surrenders. The subaltern breaks down and
implores his commandant to save his life. I imagine that
the commandant would reply, firmly but gently, that
surrender is impossible. But suppose the subaltern were his
beloved younger brother, or his only son. I can imagine that
then the commandant would reply to his son's appeal by
passionate denunciation, telling him that he is a disgrace
to the family. To discuss the matter calmly would lead to
the surrender which he knows he must not make: his instinct
would tell him that.'*

* In this situation, the decision of the commandant would presumably
be generally applauded. In spite of the tragedy, it would be in terms of
values understood by the audience. Yet the values involved are conventional human ones and some might (I think rightly) endorse E. M.
Forster's memorable (in 'What I Believe' in *Two Cheers for Democracy*).
'If I had to choose between betraying my country and betraying my
friend, I hope I should have the guts to betray my country.' In Isabella's
case the values are supernatural and imperative and admit – for a
Catholic nun – no alternative.

And this appeal to family honour is the only appeal to which Claudio is likely to respond. At the beginning (using the image which St Thomas More used as he saw the Carthusian martyrs dragged in agony to death), Claudio has said:

> If I must die,
>> I will encounter darkness as a bride
>> And hug it in mine arms,

to which Isabella has replied

>> There spake my brother; there my father's
>>> grave
>> Did utter forth a voice!

The Duke (as Friar Lodowick), in the wonderful speech beginning: 'Be absolute for death' has preached to Claudio 'the most eloquent Sermon Against the Fear of Death that has ever been written since Lucretius completed his Third Book.' But as Claudio weakens in his resolution and Isabella's is strained to its last thread, how can she better deal with it than by her 'terrible' reply:

> O you beast!
> O faithless coward! O dishonest wretch!
> Wilt thou be made a man out of my vice?
> Is't not a kind of incest to take life
> From thine own sister's shame? What should I think?
> Heaven shield my mother play'd my father fair,
> For such a warped slip of wilderness
> Ne'er issued from his blood. Take my defiance;
> Die, perish! might but my bending down
> Reprieve thee from they fate, it should proceed:
> I'll pray a thousand prayers for thy death –
> No word to save thee.*

* It is Isabella's strength here and in other speeches that puts her apart from such heroines as Ophelia, Desdemona and Cordelia and it is significant that Jack Wilson, who 'created' Isabella, had played both Ophelia and Desdemona but, in *King Lear*, played not Cordelia but Goneril.

And she is successful. When the Duke enters to tell Claudio
that there is no hope for him, he is once more in command
of himself: 'Let me ask my sister pardon. I am so out of love
with life that I will sue to be rid of it.'

Throughout the play, especially in the relationship of the
Duke with Angelo and in Isabella's plea for mercy for the
man who has subjected her to such bitterness, the theological issues are made explicit. The directness of Isabella's
plea for mercy couched specifically (as Portia's is not and,
of course, cannot be) in Christian terms:

> Alas, alas!
> Why all the souls that were, were forfeit once;
> And He that might the vantage best have took
> Found out the remedy. How would you be
> If He, which is the top of judgment, should
> But judge you as you are? O, think on that,
> And mercy then will breathe within your lips
> Like man new-made:

and the comparison between Divine and human power:

> O it is excellent
> To have a giant's strength; but it is tyrannous
> To use it like a giant . . . Merciful Heaven,
> Thou rather with thy sharp and sulphurous bolt
> Split'st the unwedgeable and gnarled oak
> Than the soft myrtle: but man, proud man,
> Dress'd in a little brief authority,
> Most ignorant of what he's most assured,
> His glassy essence, like an angry ape
> Plays such fantastic tricks before high heaven
> As make the angels weep

are two of the best known The picture of the fallen world,
the Vienna, saturated with a sexual corruption which is to
'boil and bubble till it o'er-run the stew' and where order
itself is overthrown

> And liberty plucks justice by the nose;
> The baby beats the nurse, and quite athwart
> Goes all decorum;

the theological precision of Angelo's

> 'Tis one thing to be tempted, Escalus,
> Another thing to fall'

expanded into, when Isabella is pleading for Angelo,

> My brother had but justice,
> In that he did the thing for which he died:
> For Angelo
> His act did not o'ertake his bad intent;
> And must be buried but as an intent
> That perish'd by the way. Thoughts are no subjects,
> Intents but merely thoughts.

and of the insistence, even in a play turning on chastity, that the sins of the flesh are less than the sins of the spirit and that unchastity 'of the deadly seven is the least,' and a host of similar examples, leave no reasonable doubt that, however differently different minds may see the play, the writer of it was a Catholic.

VIII : Historical Perspective

THE evening before the execution of Mary Queen of
Scots she asked to be allowed the consolation of her own
chaplain. This was refused, although he was in the castle,
by one of the commissioners for the execution, the Earl of
Kent, a convinced and fiery Anglican. He told the Queen
'that her life would have been the death, as her death would
be the life' of English Protestantism. She was sufficiently
impressed by this to say at supper to her physician, Burgoin:
'Here comes the truth at last. They told me I was to die
because I had plotted against the Queen; but then arrives
this Kent whom they sent hither to convert me and what says
he? I am to die for my religion.' Mary, however, had one
consolation in death. Anticipating the probable situation
the Pope had sent her a consecrated Host, which she kept in
a gold ciborium, that if a priest were denied her she might
administer the Blessed Sacrament to herself. Thus fortified,
she faced the scaffold.

After the Commission for her execution had been read –
to which she listened 'with as small regard as if it had not
concerned her at all and with as cheerful a countenance as
if it had been a pardon' – the Dean of Peterborough started
to preach a sermon to her. She interrupted him with: 'Mr
Dean, I am settled in the ancient Catholic Roman religion,
and mind to spend my blood in defence of it.' 'Mr Dean
said,' continues the eyewitness account, 'change your opinion
and repent you of your former wickedness and settle your
faith only in Jesus Christ, by Him to be saved.' Then she
answered again and again: 'Mr Dean trouble not yourself

any more, for I am settled and resolved in this my religion and am purposed therein to die.' Then the Earl of Shrewsbury and the Earl of Kent, perceiving her so obstinate, told her that since she would not hear the exhortation begun by Mr Dean, 'We will pray for Your Grace that you may have your heart lightened, even at this last hour, with the true knowledge of God, and so die therein.' Then she answered: 'If you will pray for me, my Lords, I will thank you: but to join in prayer with you I will not, for that you and I are not of one religion.'

'Then the Lords called for Mr Dean, who, kneeling on the scaffold stairs, began this prayer: "O most gracious God and merciful Father etc." all the assembly, saving the Queen of Scots and her servants, saying after him. During the saying of which prayer, the Queen of Scots, sitting upon a stool, having about her neck an *Agnus Dei*,* in her hand a crucifix, at her girdle a pair of beads with a golden cross at the end of them, a Latin book in her hand, began with tears and with loud and fast voice to pray in Latin; and in the midst of her prayers she slided off from her stool, and kneeling said divers Latin prayers; and after the end of Mr Dean's prayer, she kneeling prayed in English to this effect: "For Christ His afflicted Church and for an end of their troubles: for her son; and for the Queen's Majesty that she might prosper and serve God aright." She confessed that she hoped to be saved "by and in the blood of Christ, at the foot of whose crucifix she would shed her blood." Then said the Earl of Kent, "Madam settle Christ Jesus in your heart and leave those trumperies." Then she little regarding, or nothing at all, went forward with her prayers, desiring that "God would avert His wrath from this island and that He would give her grief and forgiveness for her sins." These, with other prayers she made in English, saying she forgave

* An *Agnus Dei* is a small disc of wax stamped with the figure of a lamb, representing Our Lord as victim. They are solemnly blessed by the Pope on the Wednesday of Holy Week. They were among the things which were specially forbidden to be brought into England at this time.

her enemies with all her heart that had long sought her
blood, and desired God to convert them to the truth; and
in the end of the prayer she desired all saints to make
intercession for her to Jesus Christ, and so kissing the crucifix,
and crossing of her also, said these words: "Even as Thy
arms, O Jesus, were spread here upon the cross, so receive
me into Thy arms of mercy and forgive me all my sins." '

The Dean of Peterborough was Dr Richard Fletcher who,
seven years later, was promoted to the Bishopric of London.
Handsome, courtly, eloquent, fond of luxury and pomp,
his life centred upon the Court and patronage; his initials,
R.F., can still be seen in the stained-glass-windows of the
Hall at Fulham Palace which he was building when he
died. But he is remembered now mainly as the father of his
more famous son, John Fletcher. John was seventeen at the
time of the Bishop's death and remained filially attached to
Anglicanism, attending his local church and having his
name entered in the 'token' books. The friend of Ben
Jonson and Massinger, he joined the King's Players as one
of the writers for their theatres the Globe and Blackfriars,
though his name neither then nor throughout posterity
stood alone. With Francis Beaumont, five years his junior,
he created a legend and a literature.

Beaumont was to write:

> What things we have seen
> Done at the Mermaid! heard words that have been
> So nimble and so full of subtle flame,
> As if that every one from whence they came
> Had meant to put his whole wit in a jest,
> And had resolved to live a fool the rest
> Of his dull life,

but perhaps after all life, for the inseparable pair, was more
potent than art. As J. St. Loe Strachey puts it in his preface
to their works: 'In the whole range of English literature,
search it from Chaucer till today, there is no figure more

fascinating or more worthy of attention than "the mysterious double personality" of Beaumont and Fletcher. Whether we bow to the sentiment of the first Editor who, though he knew the secret of the poets, yet, "since never parted while they lived," "conceived it not equitable to separate their ashes" and so refuse to think of them apart; whether we adopt the legendary union of the comrade poets who dwelt on the Bankside, who lived and worked together, their thoughts no less in common than the cloak and the bed o'er which tradition has grown fond; whether we think of them as of two minds so married that to divorce or disunite them were a sacrilegious deed . . . whether we treat the poets as a mystery to which love and sympathy are the initiation, or as a problem for the tests and reagents of critical analysis to solve, the double name of Beaumont and Fletcher will ever strike the fancy and excite the imagination more than most other names in the annals of English song.'

The King's Players had already produced their *Philaster*, *The Maid's Tragedy* and *King and no King*, alternating with Shakespeare's *Cymbeline*, *The Winter's Tale* and *The Tempest*, when, in 1613, Beaumont decided to marry for money – an event which he survived only three years. And in 1613, Fletcher collaborated with Shakespeare, now in retirement at Stratford, in *Henry VIII*.

On stylistic grounds alone, literary critics have endorsed Dr Johnson's judgment that Shakespeare was responsible only for the scenes in which Catherine of Aragon appears – 'the genius of Shakespeare comes in and goes out with Katharine,' – and these scenes are so unmistakably Catholic in their treatment of the royal divorce which was the occasion of the Reformation that they support the theory that Shakespeare, after Speed's attack on the 'papist and his poet'* in 1611, had decided to compromise no further. Yet, if *All is True* (the title under which *Henry VIII* was first performed) were to be produced it must conform with the

* See p. 21.

conventional Protestant viewpoint and it was left to Fletcher
to supply the praise and portrait of Cranmer with which
the play ends and which so confuses the artistic unity of the
work. As the part of Cranmer was played by the actor
whose line was courtly flatterers, princely in appearance, one
may speculate on how far Fletcher drew on his father as a
model. But about Shakespeare's sympathies in the matter
there can be no possible doubt. Quite apart from his portrait
of Catherine, he departs both from his usual sources and
from the prevailing temper of the time by making Henry
capricious, despotic, brutal and the slave of his passions.
His audacity in this has made one critic remark that 'seeing
what Shakespeare might have made of him as the founder of
Protestantism, this play furnishes the strongest proof of
Shakespeare's Catholic sympathies.'

There is another and a different pointer. The description
of Wolsey given to Catherine by her servant Griffith runs:

> He was a scholar and a ripe and good one;
> Exceeding wise, fair-spoken, and persuading;
> Lofty and sour to them that loved him not;
> But to those men who sought him sweet as summer.
> And though he were unsatisfied in getting –
> Which was a sin – yet in bestowing, madam,
> He was most princely. Ever witness for him
> Those twins of learning which he raised in you,
> Ipswich and Oxford! one of which fell with him,
> Unwilling to outlive the good that did it;
> The other, though unfinished, yet so famous,
> So excellent in art, and still so rising,
> That Christendom shall ever speak his virtue.
> His overthrow heaped happiness upon him;
> For then and not till then he felt himself
> And found the blessedness of being little:
> And to add greater honours to his age
> Than man could give him, he died fearing God.

That this is based on the following description can hardly be doubted: 'Exceeding wise, fair-spoken, high-minded, full of revenge, vicious of his body: lofty to his enemies, were they never so big; to those who accepted and sought his friendship, wonderful courteous a ripe schoolman . . . insatiable to get and more princely in bestowing, as appeareth by his two colleges at Ipswich and Oxford, the one over-thrown by his fall, the other unfinished and (as yet, as it lieth) for an house of students – considering all the appurtenances – incomparable through Christendom; never happy till his overthrow wherein he showed such moderation and ended so perfectly that the hour of his death did him more honour than all the pomp of his life past.'

This particular passage is from Blessed Edmund Campion's *History of Ireland*, cited in Holinshed's *Chronicles*.

It is beyond question that the main source for Shake-speare's historical plays was Raphael Holinshed's *The Chronicles of England, Scotland and Ireland* of which a reprint appeared in 1587. But Holinshed himself owed much to an earlier history, first published in 1548, known as Hall's *Chronicle – The Union of the Noble and Illustre Famelies of Lancastre and York* – which was a piece of fervent Protestant propaganda designed to justify any repressive measures of Henry VIII as preferable to a renewal of the strife of factions. So bitterly anti-Catholic was Hall that, when England again had a Catholic sovereign in Mary I, the first edition was almost entirely destroyed. Holinshed, writing thirty years later, to a large extent based himself on Hall, in some cases copying him verbatim. More importantly, Shakespeare, though using Holinshed as his main source, occasionally used Hall as the direct source of various passages (for example the scene in *Richard II* – V. 2 – between the Duke and Duchess of York and their son Aumerle.)*

In 1940 a copy of Hall came into the possession of Alan

* The evidence will be found in detail in Dr Gordon Zeeveld's *The Influence of Hall on Shakespeare's Historical Plays* (1936).

Keen and Roger Lubbock which contained manuscript marginal annotations by the original owner, running to three thousand six hundred words. For fourteen years, the possessors of the copy pursued their researches and in *The Annotator* (1954) showed the probability – to put it at its lowest – that it was the copy owned by the young Shakespeare. They had, indeed, announced it at the outset, but as the late A. P. Rossiter wrote in the *Durham University Journal* for March 1941: 'It is a misfortune of war that Mr Alan Keen's discovery of "several hundred annotations" in the margins of an old black-letter history book should have received so slight and so passing attention in the press.' The subsequent neglect of the discovery is probably due to the fact that, if it is indeed Shakespeare's copy, it proves beyond any doubt that he was a Catholic. In the margin against Hall's propaganda outbursts against 'proud priors,' for example, he wrote succinctly enough: 'Allways lying.'

It must be admitted that part of the authors' theory seems unnecessarily strained, if not untenable. They suggest that in 1578 John Shakespeare, in order to have his son brought up in a Catholic household, sent him as a singing-boy to Lea Hall in Lancashire, the home of Alexander Houghton who, in his will of 1581, refers to a 'William Shakeshafte now dwelling with me.' On this theory, William Shakespeare would have returned to Stratford in 1582 for his marriage to Anne Hathaway and left in 1585 to join the players of Sir Thomas Hesketh whom Houghton had asked to look after 'William Shakeshafte.' As Shakeshafte was a reasonably common Lancashire name and as the Somerville affair of 1583 provides an adequate enough historical reason for William Shakespeare leaving Stratford, this theory seems to me unlikely in the extreme. But the more important point is that this suggestion has, in fact, nothing to do with the probability of the marginal notes in the copy of Hall's *Chronicles* being in Shakespeare's handwriting, for this depends not at all on hypothetical journeyings in Lancashire and a change of name, but on H. T. F. Rhodes's thirteen-page scientific analysis of the handwriting itself, reinforced by Shakespeare's religious bias and political selectivity in the 'history plays.'

Mr Rhodes (who is the calligraphic expert officially employed in both London and Paris) writes: 'Though it is difficult to make any valid comparison between Shakespeare's known hand and these notes, because of the disparity in quantity and because of the pronounced change in Shakespeare's hand in his last years, yet certain "individual characteristics" appear in all his writing; and these characteristics also appear in the annotations. The differences between Shakespeare's hand and the Annotator's are all differences in design and not such as to prove a difference of authorship. The similarities, which are all "individual characteristics" are for that reason more significant, and indicate the probability that Shakespeare and the Annotator were the same man.'

The evidence of the 'history-plays' for Shakespeare's Catholicism has been exhaustively examined in H. Muntschmann and K. Wentersdorf's *Shakespeare and Catholicism*.* Here it may suffice to take one play, *King John*, which some commentators have seen as anti-Catholic or at least anti-Papal. Of King John's speech:

> No Italian priest
> Shall tithe or toll in our dominions;
> But as we, under Heaven, are supreme head,
> So under him, that great supremacy,
> Where we do reign, we will alone uphold,
> Without th' assistance of a mortal hand:
> So tell the Pope; all reverence set apart
> To him and his usurp'd authority.

* Published in New York in 1952, this valuable book has not yet been published in England, though an adequate summary of its main findings forms an appendix of M. D. H. Parker's *The Slave of Life*.

One critic has written that it is 'much stronger evidence against Roman sympathies in the poet than Friar Laurence, or anybody else, can be in their favour' and even Mr Ivor Brown 'feels a pressure of conviction and even of real glee behind the defiant lines.'

On this particular point it may be sufficient answer to say that the lines are put into the mouth of King John, who is represented as a tyrant, a coward, an oath-breaker and a murderer and who himself has 'usurped authority' from the legitimate heir of England. As Shakespeare is a dramatist, the speech is appropriate to the speaker and it would be as wrong to attribute 'real glee' to the author here as it would be in the case of the opposing sentiments in which the Cardinal-Legate Pandulph describes John's change of heart:

> King John hath reconciled
> Himself to Rome; his spirit is come in
> That so stood out against the Holy Church,
> The great metropolis and see of Rome.

In each case, the attitude is what might be expected from the historical character and is no indication of the author's mind.

Nevertheless the play as a whole affords a very clear indication of Shakespeare's convictions. *King John* is based not directly upon any chronicles but upon an earlier play *The Troublesome Raigne of King John* which was printed in 1591, five or six years before Shakespeare's play. Professor Dover Wilson is of the opinion that 'nothing is more remarkable than the evident pains taken by Shakespeare to rid the play of the anti-Catholic bias of his predecessors.' Liebermann goes further and considers the changes as 'systematic censorship' in the Catholic interest. For example, the earlier author, describing John's decision to finance his expedition by impounding Church property, writes:

> I'll seize the lazy abbey-lubbers' lands
> Into my hands to pay my men of war.
> The pope and popelings shall not grease themselves
> With gold and groats that are the soldiers' due.

Shakespeare changes this to

> Our abbeys and our priories shall pay
> This expedition's charge.

In the *Troublesome Raigne*, the King, after the defeat of the French, refers to

> The arch-proud titled priest of Italy
> That calls himself grand vicar under God

and, after suggesting that the Pope has called him an ass, says that the description is more appropriate to the monarchs on the Papal side:

> The title – reverently might I infer –
> Became the kings that erst have borne the load,
> The slavish weight of that controlling priest.

This Shakespeare omits altogether, as he does John's defiance of his excommunication: 'So, sir, the more the fox is cursed the better he fares: if God bless me, let the Pope and his shavelings curse and spare not.'

Two popular anti-Catholic scenes in the old play find no place in *King John* – one in which a nun is discovered hidden in a monastery and the situation is exploited to defame monastic institutions; the other, which occupies seven or eight pages, concerning a monk who is to kill the king, is blessed by the abbot, given absolution in advance and promised that masses will be offered for his soul every month. The King, dying, remarks:

> This is the fruit of popery, when true kings
> Are slain and shoulder'd out by monks and friars

and his avenger, killing the Abbot, exclaims:

> There lie the abbot, abbey-lubber, devil.
> March with the monk unto the gates of hell.

At the very end of *King John* are the ringing lines:

> Come the three corners of the world in arms,
> And we shall shock them. Nought shall make us rue
> If England to itself do rest but true

in place of *The Troublesome Raigne*'s

> Let England live but true within itself,
> And all the world can never wrong the state . . .
> If England's peers and people join in one,
> Nor Pope, nor France, nor Spain can do them wrong.

There are many other instances of this pro-Catholic 'censorship' being exercised at varying points – some theological, as about the nature of absolution; some historical, as about the reason for the English desertion of John; some dramatic – but enough has been said to suggest that *King John* and *Henry VIII*, far from establishing, as they are so often said to do, that Shakespeare was an enthusiastic Protestant, confirm, perhaps more certainly than any other plays in the canon, that his historical perspective was that of a Catholic.

IX: Priest, Parson and Holy Writ

IN the historical plays Shakespeare, when depicting the great ecclesiastics of the past, remains faithful to his sources. Wolsey, Pandulph, Beaufort, Chichele (the Archbishop of Canterbury in *Henry V*) and the various Bishops who play their partisan parts in the struggle for power between York and Lancaster are drawn as they were, 'good' or 'bad.' In the comedies and tragedies, on the other hand, Shakespeare when drawing a religious gives rein to his own imagination – the Franciscans in *Measure for Measure*, Friar Laurence in *Romeo and Juliet* (though this may be a portrait of Father John Frith), Friar Francis in *Much Ado about Nothing*, the chaplain in *Twelfth Night*, the Abbess Aemilia in *The Comedy of Errors*. In every case the portrayal is sympathetic, as it is even of those mentioned only in absence, like the old hermit who converts the usurping Duke in *As You Like It*.

The Anglican clergy, on the other hand, are treated very differently. William Addison, in *The English Country Parson*, remarks: 'The parson, strangely enough, was not a favourite character with Shakespeare. His best cuts a poor figure. Perhaps the one who springs first to mind is the Welsh parson Hugh Evans in *The Merry Wives of Windsor* . . . In *Love's Labour's Lost*, the parson, Sir Nathaniel, is referred to as "a foolish, mild man; an honest man, look you, and soon dashed. He is a marvellous good neighbour, faith, and a very good bowler." He counted for little. It seems difficult to understand why Shakespeare did not make more use of the Church, already so rich in personalities.'

Yet, if one may believe the *Survey of the State of the Ministry in Warwickshire*, drawn up by the authorities in 1586, Shakespeare was reporting only what he saw. The Vicar of Claverdon, for instance, is described as: 'A dumb and un-learned hireling, a very disordered person, a common jester and alehouse haunter, a shifter, a buyer and seller of land: he once laid the communion cup to pawn.' The Vicar of Wooton was 'a preacher, though he be grown idle, negligent and slothful; a man defamed and of tainted life.' The Vicar of Barford was 'a dumb hireling, unlearned; a man given to idleness and gaming; of tainted and vicious life; there are great presumptions that he holdeth the benefice by simony.' The Vicar of Lapworth (where the Catesbys held property) was 'neither preacher nor good reader; of ruffianly be-haviour and of suspected life; one that playeth the serving-man in a livery coat, sometime the minister; he is but an hireling to one that hath the parsonage in farm.' And so examples might be multiplied.

It is not to be doubted that this state of affairs greatly troubled the Anglican authorities; it is certain that there were many good exceptions to this lamentable picture. But it is noteworthy that Shakespeare did not avail himself of the exceptions and by his four great portraits – Sir Hugh Evans, Sir Nathaniel, Sir Oliver Martext in *As You Like It* and Sir Topas, the curate in *Twelfth Night* – he was at pains to present the Established clergy in an unfavourable light. Without knowledge of the historical background one might almost suspect them of being caricatures; but, as Rev. Ronald Bayne has put it in *Shakespeare's England*, 'Shake-speare's "Sir Johns"* reflect very accurately the type of parish priest common in his day.' And J. H. de Groot in *The Shakespeares and the 'Old Faith'* draws the conclusion:

---

* 'Sir John' was a contemptuous term for a parish clergyman. The prefix 'Sir' is the equivalent of the modern 'Rev' in the case of the parsons – a point which Shakespearean producers often fail to recognise. Sir Hugh Evans is often treated by them as if he were a knight.

'Here and there in the plays one finds positive indications of Shakespeare's esteem for the Old Faith. First, there is the fact that Shakespeare treats the Catholic clergy more respectfully than the Protestant . . . No priest is presented in a ridiculous light. On the other hand, there is not a Protestant parish priest who is not made to appear a little ludicrous.'

Neither Sir Nathaniel nor Sir Hugh Evans are ever asked to perform any spiritual functions – it would almost be an unpleasant shock if they were – while Sir Oliver Martext's services at a marriage are refused – Touchstone's comment being 'A most wicked Sir Oliver . . . a most vile Martext' – and Sir Topas is associated with a farcical parody of an exorcism. And Sir Hugh Evans's attitude to the Bible is emphasised not only in mixing up some verses from the Psalms with a love-song, but with his inability to recognise Pistol's allusion to: 'He that hath ears to hear, let him hear' and reply: 'The tevil and his tam! What phrase is this "He hears with ear?" Why, it is affectations.'

The nature of Shakespeare's own knowledge of the Bible is still a matter of controversy, though it is unlikely that it will be more exhaustively treated than in Richmond Noble's *Shakespeare's Biblical Knowledge* (1935). Mr Noble is at pains to correct at least one legend – that Shakespeare studied the Bible at school rather in the compulsory manner in which it is studied today. Like so many historical in-accuracies, this anachronism has been given currency by Sir Sidney Lee. It was not until 1604 – the year in which King James ordered the preparation of the 'Authorised Version' – that the Bible was officially fixed as a school subject and, as Mr Noble has pointed out, 'there has been as yet no adequate proof adduced that the English Bible was taught generally in country schools between 1572 and 1580 . . . Sir Sidney Lee took it for granted that he was instructed in the Bible at school. Unfortunately this view seems to have been based on nothing more substantial than a confident assumption; there is nothing to show that he took any special pains to confirm it by means of enquiry.' It is possible, of course, that portions of Scripture may have been read at school. In this case 'then beyond all reasonable doubt the version used would have been the Genevan.'

The Genevan Bible* had been produced by a group of extreme Protestants in 1560 as a scholarly revision of the 'Great Bible' of Henry VIII's day which was still the official version read in church. The Genevan became popular with the more puritanically-minded Anglicans and, partly because its sale was enthusiastically pushed, partly because it was small and cheap, it became the most widely circulated edition. It was, in its marginal notes, markedly anti-Catholic and pro-Puritan, but – to quote Mr Noble – 'preachers, whether of the Puritan party or not, on account of its convenient size for use in the pulpit often took their texts from it. It was the Bible for family and private use and its possession was no badge of party.'

In an attempt to show that Shakespeare used the Genevan Bible, many authors have cited it as the source for his Biblical references without noticing that the particular renderings are common to other Anglican versions (as in the passage in *The Merchant of Venice* describing Jacob's battle with Laban taken from the thirtieth chapter of Genesis) and, more importantly, that the Genevan version is sometimes the same as the Rheims version of 1582.

The Rheims version was the first independent translation since 1526. It was made by members of the Jesuit seminary at Rheims and was, as Catholic Bibles (the 'Douai' version and the modern 'Knox' version) still are, from the Vulgate – the Latin translation from the original Greek and Hebrew made by St Jerome. The reason, both then and now, for the choice of the Vulgate was and is that the Greek manuscripts extant are so corrupt that they no longer agreed

---

* In a later century it was known as 'the Whig Bible' owing to a misprint in the 1562 edition, 'Blessed are the placemakers.'

D

with the version known to the Fathers of the Church, that many known to St Jerome have disappeared and that, though the Vulgate was only a translation, yet it represents contact with Greek manuscripts more ancient than any other available. Moreover, Beza, the great Protestant scholar, was in agreement with Catholic scholars on this point at least. He preferred the Vulgate to any other source for the text and there were many cases where the Genevan translation and the Rheims translation agreed with each other but disagreed with current Anglican translations.*

One of these passages, for instance, is in the parable of the Prodigal Son, where both versions have 'the husks' that the swine ate where the other renderings had 'cods.' Another is the passage in Romans where the strong are bidden to bear the 'infirmities' of the weak – instead of 'frailness.' A third is the promise that even a sparrow shall not 'fall to the ground' (instead of 'light on the ground') without God's providence being aware of it. Thus when Falstaff speaks of his 'hundred and fifty tattered prodigals lately come from swine-keeping, from eating draff and husks'; when Cassius tells Brutus that 'a friend should bear his friend's infirmities: when Hamlet sees 'a special providence in the fall of a sparrow,' these are not necessarily indications, as they are cited as being, that Shakespeare used the Genevan version. They could as easily support the more likely theory that, as a Catholic, he was familiar with the Rheims.

The Rheims version, which was brought in by the Jesuit missionaries in the early '80's, was, of course, proscribed and oaths taken on it were declared invalid. If the Shakespeares possessed a copy it would be one of the things, like the Spiritual Will, to be hidden in the house-searching of the

* The Rheims translators did not, of course, ignore the existing Greek versions. As Noble points out: 'While they translated from the Latin, it is abundantly evident, not only from their margin but also from their skilful management of the Greek definite article, that they had the Greek before them. They were, in fact, Greek scholars of no mean order.'

autumn of 1583. Mr Noble points out that 'the extent of its circulation was very restricted' and though 'there are specks of evidence in favour of that version in *All's Well* and *The Tempest*,' he finds 'no substantial evidence that Shakespeare ever quoted from it.' And, of course, unless Shakespeare was a Catholic, there was no reason for his acquaintance with a version whose circulation was not only 'restricted' but whose possession was dangerous. On the other hand, if he was, it was the one version which he might be expected to know.

In an analysis of this kind, there is always the danger of assuming the too-great exclusiveness of any one version. It is usually in *minutiae* that translations differ. When, as in the three cases I have cited, the Genevan and Rheims agree with each other and disagree with the rest, it may be assumed that Shakespeare was familiar with one or the other or both. But in the hundreds of instances which are common to all versions, it has been too easy for commentators to postulate that an 'Anglican' Shakespeare used an Anglican version and to quote that only. For example, in *Measure for Measure* (Shakespeare's only 'Biblical' title), of twenty passages based on New Testament quotations which Noble lists, all are as applicable to the Rheims as to any other translation and one – Claudio's words:

> The words of heaven: on whom it will, it will:
> On whom it will not, so; yet still 'tis just –

is nearer to the Rheims than to any other.

There are, however, occasions where the Rheims version alone matches Shakespeare's usage. The 'specks' of *The Tempest* and *All's Well* appear, on examination, not quite so small. In the former, the example is the only New Testament* quotation (if one excepts the suggestion – surely text-searching run mad – that Caliban's 'sometime am I

* The Old Testament presents a different problem. The Catholic translation, published at Douay, did not appear till 1609–10).

all wound with adders who with cloven tongues do hiss me into madness' is to be associated with the descent of the Holy Ghost in 'cloven tongues of fire,' accompanied by the information that the Rheims version uses 'parted' instead of 'cloven'). The occasion of the accepted quotation is when Ariel describing the shipwreck uses a phrase which St Paul uses on his shipwreck. Ariel's 'not a hair perished' is paralleled by the Rheims: 'There shall not a hair of the head perish of any of you.' (In all other versions it is 'fall' not 'perish.') And in *All's Well*, when the Clown says: 'I am for the house with the narrow gate . . . but many will be for the flowery way that leads to the broad gate and the great fire,' 'narrow' and 'broad' are not Shakespeare's adaptation of the 'strait' and 'wide' gates which are so familiar (and which are used in every version) but the Rheims rendering, which reads: 'Enter ye by the narrow gate, because broad is the gate . . .'

Another such instance of particularity, to which Mr Noble does not refer in his exhaustive analysis but which is certainly evidence for the Rheims, whether 'substantial' or not, is the use of the word 'cockle' instead of 'tares' in the parable of the Wheat and the Tares. No other version but the Rheims (as the Catholic 'Douai' today) uses 'cockle' and even at the present time it is possible to identify a born Catholic by this particular usage.* In *Love's Labour's Lost* there is the sentence, 'sowed cockle, reaped no corn.'

It seems not unreasonable, therefore, to infer that when Shakespeare's mind turned to the Bible for illustrations, the words and phrases which occurred to his memory were those with which he was most familiar in the version he knew – the Catholic translation which, from the time when he was eighteen, men had risked their lives to distribute and to read.

---

* Not a convert, who may be more used to the otherwise universal 'tares.' If any reader is sceptical, I suggest that he make the experiment.

X : Blackfriars

THE production of *Henry VIII* marked the end of the Globe, through circumstances no one had foreseen. Sir Henry Wotton, writing to Sir Edmund Bacon on July 2, 1613, described them: 'The King's players had a new play, called *All is True*, representing some principal pieces in the reign of Henry VIII, which was set forth with many extraordinary circumstances of pomp and majesty, even to the matting of the stage; the Knights of the Order with their Georges and garters, the Guards with their embroidered coats and the like: sufficient, in truth, within a while to make greatness very familiar if not ridiculous. Now, King Henry making a masque at the Cardinal Wolsey's house, and certain chambers being shot off at his entry, some of the paper, or other stuff, wherewith one of them was stopped, did light on the thatch, where being thought at first but an idle smoke, and their eyes more attentive to the show, it kindled inwardly, and ran round like a train, consuming in less than an hour the whole house to the very grounds.' From this time, the King's Players had to content themselves with their small indoor theatre in Blackfriars.

The precinct of Blackfriars, lying between Ludgate Hill and the River Thames had been, in pre-Reformation times, the property of the Dominican (or Black) Friars. Here was the Priory, with all its buildings; the church; the Prior's lodging, sufficiently imposing for Henry VIII to lodge the Emperor Charles V in. In Blackfriars, Parliament had sat and here, too, had been held the actual trial of Catherine of Aragon which Shakespeare had represented on the stage.

With its shops and houses occupied by notable servants of church and state, and its walls, with four gates to shut it off from the City which had no jurisdiction over its 'liberty,' it was a place of sanctuary as well as importance.

After the Reformation and the destruction of the monastery, Blackfriars became an exclusive residential district for 'noblemen and gentlemen.' On Shakespeare's arrival in London, the list of persons 'as well honourable as worshipful inhabiting the precincts' included the Earl of Lincoln, Lord Cobham, Lord de la Warr, Lord Clinton, Lord Buckhurst, the Lord Chief Justice of England, the Master of the Rolls, the Queen's Solicitor and others of similar distinction. Among the lesser residents was Shakespeare's schoolfellow at Stratford, Richard Field, who was apprenticed to the French printer, Thomas Vautrollier, and, in 1588, married his widow, succeeded to the business and in due course published *Venus and Adonis* and *The Rape of Lucrece*.

There was also a discreet theatre established in the old chapter house where the boy-actors – the choristers attached to St Paul's and the Chapel Royal – rehearsed for their Court productions of Lyly's plays. According to their lease, it was for rehearsals only; but, inevitably, they started to give public performances and the landlord, complaining that they had ruined the amenities of the neighbourhood, turned them out in 1584.

Twelve years later, in 1596, a theatre was again planned. James Burbage, discovering that the lease of his Theatre in Shoreditch was not to be renewed on economic terms when it expired the following year, set about to find a new site. He decided on Blackfriars, as being immune from interference by the City authorities, and purchased one of the old buildings (possibly that which had been used by Sir Thomas Cawarden as a storeplace for equipment used for the Revels), and had spent a considerable sum in converting it into a theatre, roofed and lighted, when he met with violent opposition from the inhabitants of Blackfriars. In the last twenty years the tone of the precinct might have a little declined, but the residents still would not tolerate a public theatre, with its 'noise of the drums and trumpets' and its audiences of 'vagrant and lewd persons' who would ruin the amenities beyond repair. Headed by Lord Hunsdon, thirty-one residents petitioned the Privy Council (Richard Field was one of the signatories) and the project was stopped. Less than two months later, James Burbage died, leaving the now useless theatre to his younger son, Richard, who at the time was playing Prince Hal in the second part of *Henry IV*.

If Blackfriars was adamant against a public* theatre, it was prepared to tolerate, as it had before, a boys' company, and in 1600 Richard Burbage let his property to a syndicate of whom one of the members was the Master of the singing-boys of the Chapel Royal. The new management commissioned Ben Jonson to write for them – *Cynthia's Revels* was his first contribution – and continued in occupation until, 1608, when, not for the first time, they irritated authority beyond the point of safety. George Chapman's *Tragedy of Byron*, which not only represented the Queen of France on the stage but showed her boxing a lady's ear, drew energetic protests from the French Ambassador, who managed to have three of the actors imprisoned – though not, to his regret, the author – and Burbage was able to buy back the lease of the theatre. He formed a new syndicate of seven – himself and his brother Cuthbert; William Shakespeare; John Hemings and Henry Condell (who were to edit the First Folio); William Sly and Thomas Evans – and, under their management, Blackfriars at last had its public theatre. This time the residents did not protest.

With the destruction of the Globe, at the ill-fated performance of *Henry VIII* on June 29, 1613, the Blackfriars was now the only theatre in which Shakespeare was a

---

* A 'public' theatre was merely one in which adult actors appeared as distinct from a 'private' one where the actors were children.

shareholder. But three months earlier he had acquired another piece of property in the precinct – the Gatehouse. And this has a significance which is not theatrical.

The Prior's Lodging, now secularised as Blackfriars' House, and its Gatehouse by the Thames had continually engaged Government attention. In the mid-eighties, one of Cecil's spies had reported: 'It has sundry back-doors and bye-ways and many secret vaults and corners. It has been in time past suspected and searched for Papists, but no good done for want of knowledge of the back-doors and bye-ways of the dark corners.' In 1589, the mansion came into the possession of the crypto-Catholic Earl of Northumberland, and the Gatehouse was let to John Fortescue, whose wife was a relative of Southampton.

The Fortescues, both Catholics, harboured many priests between 1591 and 1598, when the place was at last raided. Father Tesimond S.J., who had just landed in England, happened to call at the Gatehouse on the following day and has left, in his autobiography, a vivid picture of the circumstances. The Jesuit's companion, also a disguised priest, had got no answer when he knocked at the door and had asked Fr Tesimond to take his place. 'As I was thoroughly inexperienced in these things,' writes Father Tesimond, 'I made no great difficulty and so I went and knocked at the door for a long time before I got any answer from any direction. At last the brother of Sir John* made his appearance. I asked him his name and then told him that my companion was not far off, giving his name, and saying that at his request I was come to give them notice of his arrival and to beg them to receive us for the night. The gentleman was astounded and for a short time kept silence, looking at

---

* Father Tesimond confused John Fortescue with his uncle, Sir John Fortescue, Queen Elizabeth's Chancellor of the Exchequer – a comprehensible mistake in the circumstances but one which has given some difficulty to early commentators, one of whom has noted it as 'most curious' that 'Sir John Fortescue's house was resorted to by priests' and has pointed out that in some points he is 'clearly mistaken.'

me fixedly and with much disdain; and at last he spoke to
me in such a way as to show that he suspected that I was a
spy or someone who had come to set a trap for him.' Father
Tesimond, however, managed to convince him of his
genuineness. 'Having received what he thought sufficient
satisfaction, he said to me that I must not be surprised at the
coldness that he had shown me, for matters were in such
straits with him and with all his family that at the first
words I spoke to him of my companion and his arrival, he
had a thousand thoughts what to say and what to think.
The very night before, he said, the whole house had been
upset, for the Queen's officers had been there with the
pursuivants in search of some priests of whom they had had
notice that they were to be found there, and that by name
they had asked for that companion of mine, who it was
said had already come back to England.

'He never remembered such a storm as they had thus had
all the night, those cursed folk having turned everything
upside down. Two or three priests were there, one of whom
was of our Society, Father Joseph Pollen by name; but by
God's favour they took none of them, as they had had time
to conceal themselves in the hiding-places that were made
on purpose for such assaults. They had, however, carried
away everything that had any sign of Catholic faith or
practice, as books, pictures, church vestments or altars.
They had also taken the master of the house, his brother,
away with them, together with his wife and children . . .
What afflicted him more than anything else was the danger
in which those young children were, in the power of those
savage wolves, and especially two little girls, who were held
to be the fairest in London.

'He ended by saying that I had indeed proved that I was
new and inexperienced in that mission by having come at
such a time, that is, openly in broad daylight, to a house
that was so well known to be Catholic, and that the danger
at that particular time was very plain and very great, on

account of the number of spies who were all about. He therefore counselled me to return, together with my companion, to some safe place, and let that storm calm down a little.'

The Fortescues and their two daughters, Elizabeth and Katherine,* were imprisoned for a time, but on their release they continued to entertain priests and other Catholics who wished for a secret meeting-place (though the 'Gunpowder Plotters' were refused on the grounds that Mistress Fortescue objected to Catesby's way of life); but eventually, to escape persecution, the Gatehouse was leased to a wealthy haberdasher, William Ireland, of whom nothing is known.

Another active Catholic in Blackfriars who also gave shelter to priests and was the object of Government suspicion, was John Robinson, a friend of the Fortescues. He died in 1613, leaving two sons, Edward and John, both devout Catholics. Edward left England to enter the English College at Rome and become a priest. John remained in Blackfriars as tenant of the Gatehouse under its new owner, William Shakespeare.

'No doubt,' writes Mr Halliday,† 'Shakespeare bought the house primarily as an investment, his only property in London, but as it was only a few yards from the Blackfriars theatre it looks as though he might have thought of living there for a time.' That, in the six months between his purchase of it and the production of the play, he wrote his scenes of *Henry VIII* there, seems more than likely. Also, whether or not it was 'primarily' an investment, its thirty years' reputation as a notorious Catholic centre can hardly have been without significance. Not only did he make a legal arrangement by which it was exempted from his 'heritable property,' but by breaking William Ireland's lease and

---

* Elizabeth married the brother of Francis Beaumont and their son, named Francis after his famous uncle, became a Jesuit: Katherine married a Bedingfield and had eleven daughters, all of whom became nuns.

† F. E. Halliday: *The Life of Shakespeare* (1961).

installing the Catholic John Robinson (whose descendants
were still living there till about 1860)* he ensured that the
Catholic tradition continued.

The inference is surely allowable that, on his periodical
visits from Stratford to London, he stayed with Robinson
at the Gatehouse and that they were on terms of friendship.
What is certain is that John Robinson was in Stratford during
Shakespeare's last illness and was one of the witnesses of
his will on March 25, 1616. He may have stayed a further
month and actually been present at the death-bed. In any
case, he was in a position to have brought a secret priest
there at any time it was deemed necessary.

Yet there is another of Shakespeare's deals in property –
an earlier one in Stratford – which suggests that such a
journey might have been unnecessary. In 1602, he bought
a cottage in Chapel Lane, a minute or two's walk from New
Place. Nothing is known of its tenant, but Sir Edmund
Chambers' comment that it was 'for the use of his gardener,
one may suppose' is the obvious explanation. And the date
of the purchase of the cottage, the year following John
Shakespeare's death, would be consonant with William's
determination that his mother, in her widowhood, should
have the consolations of her religion without any difficulty –
for it should be unnecessary to stress at this point that almost
the stock disguise for a priest in a recusant family during all
these years was a gardener.

This is no more than a guess, but at least it is not a
romantic guess, but one based on known historical probabilities and admitted customs of time and place. Either
because he had a resident priest of his own or through the
good offices of his Catholic friend and tenant in London,
whose brother was a priest, Shakespeare could, beyond any

* Though the actual house was destroyed in the Fire of London, the
new one was built on the exact spot and, according to John Timbs in
his *Curiosities of London* published in 1867 'until these few years had been
tenanted by the Robinson family to whom Shakespeare leased it.'

reasonable doubt, have had a priest at his death-bed to give him the Last Sacraments and to ensure, by the conventional two-shroud method of burial, that his body would lie in consecrated ground, wherever he might be officially interred.

But would it be allowed? Or would the doctor and the Anglican vicar, the two persons in attendance at a death-bed who in normal circumstances would make such consolation impossible to Catholics, obstruct it by threatening the family to lay information about it?

XI : The Doctor and the Vicar

Dr John Hall was Shakespeare's son-in-law and of him we know more than of any other member of the family. The son of a Worcestershire gentleman, he was sent to Oxford where he obtained his M.A. at the age of twenty-two and proceeded to the Continent to continue his studies in medicine. He obtained a foreign degree and in the summer of 1607, at the age of thirty-two, married Shakespeare's elder daughter, Susanna. He was only twelve years younger than his father-in-law and it is presumed that he attended him in that period of stress and illness through which he passed about that time – the period of *Timon of Athens* and *Pericles*, after his mother's death in 1608. Some see, I think rightly, a portrait of Dr Hall in Cerimon in *Pericles*:

> I   ever
> Have studied physic, through which secret art,
> By turning o'er authorities, I have –
> Together with my practice – made familiar
> To me and to my aid the blest infusions
> That dwell in vegetives, in metals, stones;
> And I can speak of the disturbances
> That nature works, and of her cures: which doth give me
> A more content in course of true delight
> Than to be thirsty after tottering honour,
> Or tie my treasure up in silken bags
> To please the fool and death.

This accords well enough with the achievements and character of one who was known as *medicus peritissimus*, 'most

skilled physician' and who, later, refused a knighthood when
it was offered him at the coronation of Charles I. Twice
when elected a Burgess of Stratford, he excused himself
on the grounds of his professional duties, in which he was
absorbed. Once more Cerimon, to whom a gentleman says:

> Your honour has through Ephesus poured forth
> Your charity, and hundreds call themselves
> Your creatures, who by you have been restored

recalls Dr Hall, with his fame and his practice extending
even beyond the boundaries of Warwickshire.

It was left on record by a contemporary, James Cooke,
who issued Hall's *Select Observations on English Bodies, and
Cures, both Empericall and Historicall* that 'even such as hated
him for his religion often made use of him.' Though some
commentators, such as Yeatman,* think that his religion
was Catholicism, this seems to me unlikely in the extreme.
All the available evidence suggests that he was a Puritan,
holding a creed which was theologically offensive to Catholics and Anglicans alike. Nevertheless his charity, his skill
and his complete trustworthiness gave him many Catholics
among his patients – Margaret Reynolds (whose will he
witnessed), Mary Talbot, Lady Smith, Lady Underhill and
others of her Catholic family; the Catholic Sheldons, Throckmortons, Combes, Nashes and Lanes; and even a recusant
priest, Father Brown, whom he noticed in his case-book as
'a Romish priest, labouring of an ungaric fever (typhoid)
in danger of death.'

It seems, therefore, quite clear that, altogether apart
from his personal relationship to the dying man, Dr John
Hall, Puritan though he was, would have been no obstacle to
Catholic rites and burial for Shakespeare. This is not to
suggest, of course, that he was actually present during them,
but only that he was aware of what was passing and could
be trusted to keep and guard the secret.

* J. P. Yeatman: *The Gentle Shakespeare* (1906).

Could the same be said about the Vicar, the Rev. John Rogers, who was also apparently a Puritan and, at least at the beginning of his career, a follower of the extremist, Cartwright?

He had arrived in Stratford in 1605. He had four children and was extremely poor, as he admitted in his somewhat acid reply to the Corporation when they ordered him to take down his pigsties in Chapel Lane (about which Shakespeare had complained): 'How far the breeding of such creatures is needful to poor housekeepers I refer myself to those who can equal my charge.' To mollify him (the year was 1613), the Corporation presented him with a new gown and hoped he would 'amend' his unspecified 'faults and failings.' He seems not to have done so and just before Shakespeare's death was provided with a thorn in his side in the shape of an energetically Puritan curate named Harris.

From the context his 'faults and failings' might be supposed to be social and economic, but there are writers who assume them to have been doctrinal and advance the theory that they were, in the words of Dr Mutschmann, 'connected with a too liberal policy in religious matters' which made him 'popular with the Catholics.' If one knew more about the circumstances of the 'excommunication' of Judith Shakespeare and her newly-wed husband, Thomas Quiney, in the March of 1616, one might have a further clue to this.* As it is, one is left to evaluate the Rev. John Rogers's attitude from what is known of his subsequent career.

* Was it, for example, something to do with the newly-imported Puritan curate? Did the curate perform the marriage despite the Vicar? Or did the curate report the Vicar to the Puritan Bishop of Worcester? More importantly, what was the 'excommunication' for? Sir Edmund Chambers says that it was because the marriage 'took place in a season prohibited by Canon Law' . . . But they were married before Lent – on the Saturday before Ash Wednesday – and in any case what is forbidden in Lent is not marriage itself (which can be celebrated at any time) but a Nuptial Mass, which is not relevant to an Anglican church.

Soon after Shakespeare's death – at the beginning of 1617 at latest – a 'confederacy' was formed against the Vicar which came to a head in 1618 when King James published his anti-Puritan *Book of Sports* permitting such 'harmless recreations' as May Games and Morris Dancing on Sundays. This crystallised, in the most practical manner, the cleavage between the sympathisers with the Catholic way of life and the Puritans. Nor did the Vicar leave any doubt where his preferences lay.

The anti-Rogers party thereupon began to canvass the claims of a fanatical young Puritan preacher from Evesham, by name Thomas Wilson, as 'successor' to John Rogers who, comprehensibly enough, had by now an overriding desire to get out of Stratford and, in 1619, accepted another incumbency. The pro-Rogers party, headed by Shakespeare's Catholic friends, John Nash and William Reynolds, decided to protest. Libels in verse and prose, containing fierce and occasionally indecent attacks on the Wilsonites, were scattered about the town and on the day of Wilson's induction, he was intercepted on the way to the church by a large and angry crowd, armed with swords, daggers, pikes and stones. Wilson was hurried into the church, the doors locked and the induction accomplished. This occurred at the beginning of June, 1619.

By the September of the same year, there was another outbreak. This time it concerned the Maypole, which the anti-Puritan party, on the strength of the King's Declaration, had managed to get erected on the road leading to the church. On the opening day of the Stratford Fair, the Bailiff – a Wilson man – had it removed, explaining that his action was not from 'any dislike unto the pole' but because it was an impediment to 'carts and carriages.' Thereupon a crowd of about forty people, which included most of the earlier rioters and the ex-Vicar, John Rogers, gathered on the road to the church and set up the pole again, with shouts of triumph. This time the Corporation reported them to the authorities on charges of 'malicious, libellous and riotous' behaviour.

The result of the Government investigation has not yet been discovered; but the subsequent history of the new Vicar is known. Wilson's passion for Puritanism went to the lengths of using the Guild Chapel for his children to play in, his servants to dry clothes in, his pigs to lie in (thereby solving the problem which had so exercised his predecessor) and his poultry to roost in 'to the further destruction of the paintings and the glass,' so that even the enthusiasm of the Corporation waned and gave place to a protest to the Bishop about his profanity.

Making all allowance for the personal factors which posterity cannot know, it would seem not unjust to assume, from these happenings, that the Rev. John Rogers was more kindly inclined to recusancy than the average non-Catholic Stratfordian and that this might well be one of his 'faults and failings' in the eyes of the Puritan-partisan Corporation. He had, it must be remembered, officiated at the burial of Shakespeare's Catholic mother in 1608 and, if her son died in the same Faith, he could refrain from intruding on the last moments at the death-bed and could turn as blind an eye to the one coffin as to the other.

The way in which a Catholic burial 'in consecrated ground' was accomplished in these years was to have two shrouds. In the second shroud was laid some earth properly consecrated by a Catholic priest and on this the corpse, already shrouded, was laid and in it wrapped. It was a token only and yet not only a token. And if Shakespeare was so 'committed to the earth' it is surely unlikely that either Dr John Hall or the Rev. John Rogers would examine the shrouding to make a report on it.

That Shakespeare was buried in Stratford Parish Church, as both his father and his mother were, is no more argument against his recusancy than against theirs. Among other known Catholics buried in the same church are William

Clopton and his wife Anne (1592 and 1596); Thomas
Reynolds and his wife Margaret (1613 and 1615); George
Badger, Shakespeare's much-persecuted neighbour in Henley
Street (1635) and the Earl and Countess of Totnes (1629
and 1637) who share an altar tomb. Moreover, Shakespeare
had in 1605 purchased the tithes that had once belonged
to the Stratford College of Priests which had been dissolved
at the Reformation. This entitled him to burial within the
chancel of the parish church, as what Bowden calls (without
underlining the irony) 'lay-Rector of Stratford.'

At this point, it may be convenient to recapitulate briefly
the evidence on which the claim for Shakespeare's Catholicism rests. There are, in his life, some certainties, some
probabilities and some possibilities. It is certain that both
his parents were open Catholics who suffered on account
of their faith, so that the probability is that, in the first
five years of his life he was brought up as any other child
would be in a devout Catholic home. If he went to school
at five, it is certain that his first schoolmaster was a Catholic.
It is also certain that from the age of seven to eleven he
was taught by a Catholic who eventually became a priest
and that among his schoolfellows was one who became both
priest and martyr. If he remained at school till he was fifteen,
his last master was a Catholic, whose younger brother was
also a martyr. It is certain that he was married by a Catholic
priest.

It is certain that, by reason of the Shakespeares' relationship with the great Catholic 'cousinage' in the Midlands –
which included the Throckmortons, the Catesbys, the
Winters, the Treshams, the Ardens, the Bushells – he was
affected by the Somerville plot and possibly on account of
it left Stratford. It is certain that the object of his literary
attack, Sir Thomas Lucy, was the chief persecutor of
Catholics in Stratford. It is possible that Lucy ordered his
imprisonment.

It is certain that his patron, Southampton, was a Catholic.

It is probable that the martyr and poet, Robert Southwell, dedicated a volume of his religious poems to Shakespeare and it is possible that this influenced *The Rape of Lucrece*.

In London we have no record, from the parish 'token' books, that Shakespeare even attended an Anglican service, though the signatures of his friends and associates are there. On the other hand we know that at some period he went to lodge in a family diplomatically immune from the penalties of non-attendance at church. We have no record, among his poems, of any mourning poem for Elizabeth I or praise of James I, such as his contemporaries profusely indulged in; this may be because no Catholic was likely to celebrate a persecuting monarch. His plays, however they are regarded, afford evidence of his understanding of Catholicism and, when considered carefully in their setting, suggest sympathy with it. It is possible that he owned a copy of Hall's *Chronicle* which he annotated in the Catholic sense: in any case, his bias in the historical plays is Catholic. It is certain that he was said to have 'died a Papist' by an early writer and he was mentioned for his Papistry by Speed during his lifetime. We know that he bought, towards the end of his life, a notorious centre of Catholic activity in London and installed in it a known and practising Catholic, who also witnessed his will. We have some evidence that he was familiar with the Catholic translation of the New Testament and we know certainly that his father copied out the 'Spiritual Will' provided for Catholics in times of persecution. It is probable that William was also acquainted with this, though there is no evidence that he personally availed himself of one. His use of the Anglican church in Stratford for the ceremonies connected with the births, marriages and deaths of his family constitutes no argument against his Catholicism in view of the conditions of the times and the nature of the services.

What does all this amount to? Obviously there is not the same kind of 'proof' that Shakespeare was a Catholic as

there is that Cardinal Newman was a Catholic. But there is
sufficient evidence on which to base a verdict (to say 'non-
proven' is not so much to give a verdict as to refuse to give
one); and Professor R. W. Chambers provides an example
which may be of help in an evaluation of this kind.

'A Jew, obviously in a state of some distress, was met by
his Rabbi, who enquired the cause. "I was called as a
witness," was the reply, "and I was fined £10." "No, no,
Abe. You mean you were called as a defendant and fined
£10." "No, I was called as a witness; and the Judge said:
'What is your name?' And I said (as you know) 'Abraham
Isaac Jacob Solomon.' And the Judge said: 'Are you a Jew?'
And I said, 'Now don't be a silly ass.' And I was fined £10." '

'Yet no one of these names is conclusive. Think of Abraham
Lincoln, Izaak Walton, Jacob Tonson, Solomon Grundy.
But most of us would agree that the *combination* suggests
Jewish origin with sufficient certainty to render the retort
upon the Judge eminently justifiable.'

Applying this example, Professor Chambers continues,
'in practice, we constantly act on the principle that several
unreliable arguments together make a reliable one. You
have to meet in a crowd a Mr Harris, hitherto unknown to
you, but who, you are informed, has red hair, wears a
monocle and walks with a limp. You would address with
some confidence a stranger possessing those characteristics;
and if he responded to the name of Harris, you would accept
the identification without brooding over the fact that there
are nearly a thousand Harrises in the London Telephone
Directory alone. *You have not got mathematical, logical certainty:
you have that approximation to certainty which satisfies us in the
actual affairs of life.*'

I leave the Professor's italics because the truth they underline is cardinal to all true scholarship in history, which can
never speak, except in minute and unimportant details,
with a 'mathematical, logical certainty.' History is life as
it has been lived at certain times by certain persons and the

business of the historian is to re-present this as accurately as he is able. In the case of Shakespeare I suggest that anyone who knows the background of his life and work is likely to assume that he was a Catholic and to lay the onus of 'proof' to the contrary on those who deny it.

XII : At the Funeral

Shakespeare was buried on April 25, two days after his death and among the mourners who watched the service or took part in it were those who made it a microcosm of English life. The Rev. John Rogers – one may safely assume in his 'new gown' – officiated, with the curate Robert Harris (himself already noted for his funeral orations) in attendance.

Of the family, Shakespeare's widow, Anne, was sixty. His bequest to her of his 'second-best bed and the furniture' (the accessories) may possibly indicate that she was infirm.* Of her, nothing is known except that her father and John Shakespeare were friends and fellow-Catholics; that she was eight years her husband's senior, survived him by seven and bore him no children after the twins, Judith and Hamnett, were born early in 1585, two and a quarter years after the marriage. When Anne died in 1623, Dr John Hall wrote on behalf of Susanna a Latin panegyric for her tomb – the doggerel 'curse,' it will be remembered, prevented Shakespeare's tomb being opened – which, though epitaphs are not necessarily trustworthy indications of true feelings, does

---

* In any case the legacy was not (as it has been interpreted by romantics) a slight. It was a mark of consideration. By common law Anne was entitled to continue living at New Place and had a life interest in a third of her husband's inheritable estates. New Place itself Shakespeare left to the Halls, so that Anne would have her elder daugher Susanna and her son-in-law the doctor, to look after her. By the clause about the bed she would also, whatever changes might be made, keep the one she was using and to which she was accustomed.

contrive to convey a sense of genuine love and genuine loss.*

The daughters and their husbands were there – Susanna 'witty above her sex' with her beloved physician and their daughter Elizabeth, who was eight; and Judith, with her less-satisfactory newly-married Thomas Quiney, vintner of *The Cage*. But Hamnett, the only son, was dead. He had died the year before Shakespeare's purchase of New Place and had been commemorated by his father in the unforgettable mourning-speech for Arthur in *King John* written that year:

> Grief fills the room up of my absent child,
> Lies in his bed, walks up and down with me,
> Puts on his pretty looks, repeats his words,
> Remembers me of all his gracious parts, ·
> Stuffs out his vacant garments with his form;
> Then have I reason to be fond of grief.

Shakespeare's three brothers, too, were dead – Gilbert, and Richard and young Edmund, who was less than five

* The epitaph ran:
> Ubera, tu mater, tu lac vitamque dedisti;
>   Vae mihi, pro tanto munere saxa dabo?
> Quam mallem moveat lapidem bonus angelus ore!
>   Exeat, ut Christi corpus, imago tua!
> Sed nil vota valent; venias cito, Christe! resurget,
>   Clausa licet tumulo, mater et astra petet.

I have given it in Latin because E. I. Fripp in *Shakespeare's Stratford* (1928) suggests that Dr Hall had read in the Vulgate how *angelus revolvit lapidem . . . ab ostio monumenti*. Fripp is careful to establish that, in his view, Dr Hall was an extreme Puritan. His suggestion is therefore significant. Catholics, of course, would know these particular passages from the Masses of Easter Eve and Easter. But, as a matter of fact, Dr Hall's verses do not seem to me to bear any particular resemblance to the Vulgate and appear to be his own composition in Latin. In English, the panegyric runs: 'Breasts, mother, milk and life thou gavest me: alas, for so great a boon shall I give thee stones? How much rather I wish the good angel to remove the stone from the mouth, thine image to come forth as did the body of Christ. Come quickly, Christ! Though shut in the tomb, may my mother rise again and seek the stars.'

years older than Hamnett. Gilbert and Richard are shadowy
Stratfordians, but 'Ned' had followed his eldest brother to
London and become an actor in the same company. When
he was nineteen he had created the part of Rosalind in
As You Like It and his brother's description paid tribute to
his complexion:

> He'll make a proper man: the best thing in him
> Is his complexion; and faster than his tongue
> Did make offence his eye did heal it up . . .
> There was a pretty redness in his lip,
> A little riper and more lusty red
> Than that mix'd in his cheek; 'twas just the difference
> Betwixt the constant red and mingled damask.

Edmund had died at the age of twenty-seven, just before the
death of his illegitimate son, and William had paid twenty
shillings for his burial in St Saviour's, Southwark, 'with a
forenoon knell of the great bell.' But Shakespeare's sister, Joan,
was there, newly widowed. Her husband, William Hart, the
hatter, had himself been buried five days earlier. Some think
that Shakespeare's own death was due to his insistence of getting up from his sick-bed to attend his brother-in-law's funeral.
This is at least as probable as the popular romantic theory
that he died from the effects of an unjudicious drinking-bout
with Ben Jonson. To Joan her brother left the use of the
Henley Street house for her lifetime – and all his clothes,
presumably for the eventual use of her three sons, William,
Thomas and Michael, the eldest of whom was sixteen.

There was the lawyer, Thomas Greene, Shakespeare's
cousin, who had been the tenant of New Place but, once
Shakespeare had come home, had moved to St Mary's
House, next to the church, where he lived in such state in
his 'pretty, neat, gentlemanlike' residence 'in a little young
orchard' as befitted the Town Clerk and Steward of Stratford who had also been Reader and Treasurer of the Middle
Temple.

There were the young Combes, William and Thomas, the present representatives of the wealthiest family in Stratford – the family which had profited most by the Reformation pillage and had steadily increased what had been taken (including the Priests' College) by speculation and usury. Their uncle, John, had become so notorious a money-lender that when he had died, two years ago, Shakespeare, drinking in a local tavern, was said to have composed an impromptu epitaph for him:

Ten in a hundred the Devil allows
But Combe will have twelve, he swears and avows.
If anyone asks who lies in this tomb,
'Oh,' quoth the Devil, ' 'tis my John o' Combe.'

The younger Combes had carried acquisitiveness further, though in a different field. They had started forcibly to enclose the common arable land and turn it into private pasture, deliberately provoking riots in their defiance of the Corporation. Into this bitter local strife, Shakespeare, acting with his cousin Greene, had during the last few months of his life entered on the side of the commoners. In his will he had left to Thomas Combe, who had recently hit and kicked a harmless shepherd, his sword. The irony was to be misunderstood. Shortly after receiving the legacy, Combe became involved in a fight with a member of the Corporation.

The most remarkable figure at the funeral, however, was 'Great Philip Macedon' – to give him his Stratfordian title – the schoolmaster, Alexander Aspinall, who seems to have suffered from the delusion that he *was* Stratford and had at least the colour for it that he had educated most of the citizens under fifty and had been, on occasion, Chamberlain, Alderman, Deputy Town Clerk, bum-bailiff and maltster. He had arrived in the town from Lancashire just before Shakespeare's marriage and twelve years later, at the age of fortytwo, had himself married a widow of Henley Street. On that occasion, William had been on a visit home

and had, so it was said, written for him a posy to give with
the gloves which he had bought for his bride at John Shakespeare's shop:

> The gift is small: the will is all,
> Alexander Aspinall.

It was the year of *Love's Labour's Lost* and Hamnett Shakespeare, at nine, was at school under Aspinall. Father and son
could share the joke of it – for the boy, like the rest of the
pupils, called it *Ass*pinall and the father turned him into
Holofernes, 'the schoolmaster exceeding fantastical, too,
too vain,' who acted Judas before the courtiers who accented
the last syllable:

> 'And so adieu, sweet Jude! Nay, why dost thou stay?'
> 'For the latter end of his name!'
> 'For the ass to the Jude, give it to him – Jud – *as* away!

Holofernes's comment: 'This is not generous, not gentle, not
humble!' may well have been Aspinall's own. The moment
was embalmed against time.

There were the tradesmen of Stratford – Henry Walker,
the mercer, whose small son, William, was Shakespeare's
godson, remembered in his will by twenty shillings in gold;
and Walker's brother-in-law, John Smith the ironmonger,
who disliked him; and George Badger, the wollendraper,
close friend of Shakespeare and his father, an avowed
Catholic who, for that reason, had been deprived of his
Aldermanic gown and only a year ago had had his house
searched by candlelight for 'massing relics,' at the cost of
2d for candles to the Corporation; and Philip Rogers, the
apothecary, who sold ale and tobacco to supplement his
normal, but not particularly lucrative, trade in pills, oil of
vitriol, aniseed, sassafras, cassis, Venice turpentine, Burgundy
pitch, precipitate cinnabar, corrosive sublimate and confec-
tions of roses. Apparently poor as he was, he managed to
send his son to Oxford where the boy became a surgeon.

It is possible that there were visitors from London, for
the time would have allowed it. To the three great actors
and business men of the Company, Richard Burbage, John
Heminges and Henry Condell, Shakespeare had left money
to buy memorial rings. And though to the important citizens
of Stratford, their names might mean little, each brought in
their turn intangible gifts which outweighed any other there.

Richard Burbage, who had created on the stage Henry V
and Romeo and Brutus and Hamlet and Othello and Angelo
and Lear and Macbeth and Antony and was to play them till
his death in 1619, established the tradition of Shakespeare's
own interpretation which, through Taylor, Betterton,
Garrick, Kean and Irving, was to reach three centuries
ahead.* Yet to see him as an interpreter only is to misunderstand and misstate that most subtle of all relationships,
the relationship between the dramatist and the actor. For
it is always, to a greater or lesser degree, a reciprocal one.
A dramatist writes for his 'star' and the 'star' to some extent
determines both the kind of part written and details of that
part. And Richard Burbage was a very great star indeed.
When he died, at the same time as Anne of Denmark, James I's
Queen, Middleton scolded the Londoners for keeping all
their grief for the actor:

> When he expires, lo! all lament the man,
> But where's the grief should follow good Queen Anne?

and the crowds in the theatre came to watch Burbage, not
to listen to Shakespeare.

So great was the care with which the author wrote for the

* Burbage 'created' the parts and trained Taylor who succeeded him
in them. Davenant, who had seen Taylor, rehearsed Betterton, whose
veteran companions instructed Garrick. The survivors of Garrick's
company communicated them to Kean, whose method was passed on
by Chippendale (Kean's Polonius) to Irving. After Irving's death, the
tradition was to a very large extent lost – though Martin Harvey
assimilated some of it and some contemporary actors show here and
there a few remnants of it.

actor that, as T. W. Baldwin has shown, whatever character
Burbage was playing was often given his own age. The
descriptions of the parts also give a picture of him. He was
small and stocky, and had run quickly to at least the appearance of fat. Even Romeo, young as he is, 'bears him like
a portly gentleman,' Henry V is 'stubborn outside with an
aspect of iron; Hamlet is 'fat,' his flesh 'too, too solid'*; he is
thirty although this does not tally with the youthful student
of the play, because Burbage was thirty when he first played
it: and four references to his 'youth' which appear in the
original quarto are omitted from the later final edition. Some
may perhaps consider these as unimportant details, but this
is not the place to analyse the effect of the actor's temperament and range on the author's construction of the part.
All that I wish to do is to suggest that 'literary' criticism
is often based on ignorance of the real conditions in which
the creation of character for the stage (the novel, of course, is
quite a different matter) takes place and that it is more
profitable, for instance, in analysing the affinities between
Brutus and Hamlet to see them both in relation to Burbage
than to indulge in speculations about Shakespeare's 'mind.'
To quote Baldwin again, 'Burbage as an actor was marked
by dignity and strength. Of pure comedy he had almost
none, his comic effects being procured by a half-satiric
contrast of high ideals turned loose to be laughed at in a
practical world, somewhat after the manner of Cervantes.'
But in Brutus and Hamlet, the 'turning loose' was tragic.

As independent evidence of Burbage's appearance there is
the quatrain:

> His stature small but every thought and mood
> Might thoroughly from the face be understood;
> And his whole action he could change with ease
> From ancient Lear to youthful Pericles

* Critics apparently unacquainted with the theatre – where the line
is necessary for the audience to get rid of its amusement at a fat Prince
of Denmark if it wishes to – suppose that it was a misprint for 'sullied.'

and various descriptions of him in the plays – for example, his:

> trick o' th' hip:
> Mark how his body's made for't.

of *As You Like It*: his 'well-knit body' and his form 'made up like Hercules' of *All's Well*; his legs like 'Westphalia gammons' of Beaumont and Fletcher's *The Captain* – help us to see him as he was in one of the brawls about the theatre, when he set about one man with a broomstick but refrained from attacking another, 'scornfully and disdainfully playing with this deponent's nose' as it was put later in court.

Richard Burbage lived all his life in St Leonard's parish, Shoreditch, where his seven children were baptised; John Heminges and Henry Condell were neighbours in the more exclusive parish of St Mary Aldermanbury, where both were active in parish affairs. Their comfortable houses, where Heminges brought up his fourteen children and Condell his nine, were not far apart and they remained friends, actors and managers of the same company, fellow trustees of the same church to the end of their lives. Heminges, the elder, played Caesar to Condell's Antony, Polonius to Condell's Horatio, Kent to Condell's Edgar and Ross to Condell's Malcolm when Burbage was creating Brutus* and Hamlet and Lear and Macbeth. Of Heminges the picture is very clear. He became the doyen of the acting profession, as well as handling all the financial affairs of his own company. In one of the commemorative verses on Burbage occurs:

> Then fear not, Burbage, heaven's angry rod
> When thy fellows are angels and old Heminges is God.

---

* This leaves no doubt about Shakespeare's intention for the 'star' of *Julius Caesar*. Nor, indeed, does the text. But modern producers have a habit of of using Antony, which unbalances the play.

The parts Heminges played – Polonius and Kent give the clue – were usually those of old men where 'whether as father, counsellor, or servant, he is usually giving advice or laying down the law' and, to quote Baldwin once more, 'when we remember Heminges's numerous family and his successful guidance of the affairs of the company, we must feel that in this line Heminges did not act: he was himself.'

No less than Burbage, though in a different way and on a smaller scale, this old, energetic white-bearded man influenced Shakespeare's creations. Polonius owes much more to Heminges than to Lord Burleigh and when it is remembered that, four years earlier, he had also played Caesar, Polonius's: 'I was killed i' the Capitol: Brutus killed me' was likely to have an overtone for the original audiences which is lost today.

Condell is a more shadowy figure than Heminges; but he too played old and courtly men – the Duke in *Measure for Measure*; the Cardinal in *The Duchess of Malfi* – and seems, on the stage as in life, an echo of his friend. He died three years before Heminges – in 1627 – and lies buried near him in the parish church of St Mary Aldermanbury they had both served so well.

In 1623, when they were the last two members of the original company still living, Heminges and Condell linked their names inseparably in another act of service. They published the great First Folio of Shakespeare's plays. 'We have but collected them,' they wrote in their dedication to the Lord Chamberlain and his brother, 'and done an office to the dead, to procure his orphans guardians; without ambition either of self-profit or fame; only to keep the memory of so worthy a friend and fellow alive as was our Shakespeare.'

XIII : 'As was our Shakespeare'

'As was our Shakespeare.' Heminges and Condell had the right to the particularity of the 'our.' They were speaking of the man who had been their fellow-actor-manager-shareholder in the theatre for quarter of a century. He indeed belonged to their world. As Professor Bentley has put it, Shakespeare 'had more kinds of connection with the company than any other man: he was actor, shareholder, patented member, principal playwright and one of the house-keepers of the Globe. Few men in theatrical history have been so completely and inextricably bound up with the affairs of an acting troupe.'

Yet less than two centuries after his death, the process of extracting him from his environment had been successful enough for Charles Lamb to lay it down 'that the plays of Shakespeare are less calculated for a performance on a stage than those of almost any other dramatist whatever'; to emphasise his belief by repetition that 'the Lear of Shakespeare cannot be acted': and to deny any affinity between Shakespeare's 'absolute mastery over the heart and soul of man' and 'those low tricks upon the eye and ear, which a player . . . can so easily compass.'

This was the beginning of a phase of 'literary' criticism which is still not altogether extinct – 'by which Shakespeare was elevated' – the words are Middleton Murry's – 'to a sphere wherein no mortal man of genius could breathe. For a dizzy moment every line that he wrote bore the authentic impress of the divine. *Efflavit deus*. In a century, from being largely beneath criticism, Shakespeare had passed to a condition where he was almost completely beyond it.' Side by side with the literary critics came the academic annotators, who are still rampant and whose zenith of recent achievement was to occupy columns and columns of the *Times Literary Supplement* canvassing the theory that in Mrs Quickly's description of Falstaff's death: 'For after I saw him fumble with the sheets and play with flowers and smile upon his fingers' ends, I knew there was but one way; for his nose was as sharp as a pen and a' babbled of green fields,' the last words should be 'a table of Greenfield' which meant a portrait of Sir Richard Grenville and that when Falstaff smiled on his fingers' ends he was really drawing attention to the last fight of the *Revenge* – the one ship against fifty-three – which happened 176 years after his death.* 'Shakespeare' has now become a kind of national industry of the non-creative and, if the phrase 'our Shakespeare' is still used, it is in the same spirit as 'our' navy or 'our' coalfields.

But the man who died at Stratford on St George's Day 1616 was an actor-dramatist, a man pre-eminently of the theatre, a man of a persecuted profession as well as of a persecuted faith. And to understand the full significance of the day Shakespeare died, it is necessary to take this into account.

So much is known about the Elizabethan literary and theatrical scene that there is a danger of obscuring the outline by the details and this description by a foreigner,† whatever its incidental inadequacies, has the merit of restoring a much-needed proportion. Shakespeare's England was, writes Stefan Zweig, 'that titanic moment which comes unexpectedly in the life of every nation as in the life of every individual when all the energies are concentrated for a mighty thrust into the eternal process of events . . . The

* This correspondence has to be read to be believed. See TLS.
† Stefan Zweig in *Conflicts*, translated by Eden and Cedar Paul (1928).

English wished to discover, to conquer, like the conquistadors
of Spain. They needed a new speech, a new energy. Betwixt
night and morning appeared the speakers of this new speech,
the poets, the dramatists and other men of letters – fifty, a
hundred, in a decade – untamed and untamable fellows,
utterly different from the court poetasters who had been
roaming through Arcadian gardens and penning versicles
about carefully selected mythological episodes. The new-
comers stormed the theatre. They forced their way into
the rough arenas which had hitherto been reserved for bear-
baiting and similar cruel sports; the trail of blood lies
across their writings . . . Each tries to outbid the others
in savagery and exuberance. Anything and everything may
be described. Incest, murder, atrocious crime, the tumult
of unrestrained human impulses celebrate their orgies in
these writings . . . It is one formidable outburst like the
explosion of a petard; but it lasts fifty years, an outrush
of blood, an ejaculation, a single prolonged outburst of
savagery . . .

'Individual voices can scarcely be heard, individual
figures can hardly be seen, in this upheaval of energy. Each
catches fire from the others: each of them learns and pilfers
from the others; all try to outdistance their rivals; and yet
they are all the spiritual gladiators of a single celebration,
unchained slaves, scourged forward by the genius of the
hour. He brings some forth from obscure kennels in the
purlieus of the town, and others of them from palaces:
Ben Jonson, whose grandfather had belonged to the border
gentry, whilst his stepfather was a master bricklayer;
Marlowe the son of a shoemaker; Massinger, son of a gentleman attached to the household of the Earl of Pembroke;
Philip Sidney whose father was lord deputy of Ireland and
lord president of Wales – and swift vortex whirls them all
together.

'One day they are famous, flush of money, admired; next
day they are impoverished like Kyd and Heywood, fall

E

down in the street fainting from hunger like Edmund Spenser. They are swashbucklers, whoremongers, play-actors, cheats; but they are poets one and all. Shakespeare is no more than the central figure among them, "the very age and body of the time." There is no ground, there is no opportunity for singling him out amid the tumult in which one work so swiftly follows another, in which one passion so stormily rages after another. Then, suddenly and palpitatingly and convulsively as it began, this most splendid eruption of mankind comes to an end; the drama is finished; England is tired out; for a hundred years thereafter the grey and mist-laden waters of the Thames flow silently over the things of the spirit. In one furious onslaught, a whole generation stormed the heights and plumbed the depths of passion. The frenzied soul has boiled over . . . All that went before in English literature was but preparatory; all that came afterwards was but a feeble imitation of this one bold leap towards the infinite.'

Stephen Gosson, the Rector of St Botolph's, Bishopgate, who was ten years older than Shakespeare, expressed a similar view at the time, though somewhat more crudely: 'The argument of tragedies is wrath, cruelty, incest, injury, murder, either violent by sword or voluntary by poison: the persons, gods, goddesses, furies, fiends, kings, queens and mighty men. The ground-work of comedies is love, cozenage, flattery, bawdry, sly conveyance of whoredom; the persons, cooks, queans, knaves, bawds, parasites, courtezans, lecherous old men, amorous young men.' He did not care much for the audiences who 'to celebrate the sabbath flock to the theatres and there keep a general market of bawdry... Every wanton and his paramour, every man and his mistress, every John and his Joan, every knave and his quean are there first acquainted.' And of the 'harlotry players' themselves, he admitted that they were not fit for any other occupation: 'Most of the players have been either men of occupations, which they have forsaken to live by playing, or common minstrels, or trained up from their childhood to this abominable exercise and have now no other way to get their living.'

This attitude is a matter of values about which it is difficult to argue. Few, perhaps, will unreservedly endorse Rupert Brooke's protest against 'the impudent attempt to thrust the filthy and degraded standards of the modern middle-class drawing-room on the clean fineness of the Elizabethans' or agree whole-heartedly that 'the Elizabethans liked obscenity; and the primness and wickedness that do not like it have no business with them.' Yet this defiant statement is not only what one would expect a young creative artist to make but it suggests the context in which Shakespeare can be appreciated with propriety. A distinction of values must, therefore, be indicated.

Few people have analysed these with more exactitude than Clive Bell. He divides those who approach art into three categories — the artists themselves; what he calls the 'aesthetes,' whom he defines as having in common with the artist the ability 'to rise on the wings of art to a world above the world of normal experience. Both are free of the world of the spirit. To this high region they attain by means of art, as some do by thought, as many do by love. And that is why they take art seriously.' The third category is what he calls the 'cultured,' to whom art is an incident – an important incident perhaps but one which does not transport them beyond this life, but which gives this life a flavour. By the 'cultured,' life is not conditioned by art, nor judged by it. 'On the contrary art, more often than not, is tried by life. Is it like life? Is it useful to life? Is it uplifting or reassuring or subversive or reactionary? Those are the questions that people who take art seriously will never ask, because they are irrelevant.'

The difficulty is that no real communication between the categories is possible. 'How should those who have never escaped to the world of absolute values and known only this world's judge by anything else? For it is a question of values; and the values of Classes A and B (artists and aesthetes) are different from those of Class C (cultured). This difference leads to a further and most unfortunate misunderstanding. Habitual visitors to the other world are apt to be somewhat critical and contemptuous of this, and what is worse, can discover no essential difference in the variety of entertainments provided this side the barrier. Hence the complaint of Class C that Classes A and B are coarse and brutal in their relaxations and sweeping in their condemnation. They are said to drink and use foul language and tell dirty stories and consort with publicans and prostitutes. When some purveyor of refined treats, Sir Nigel Playfair for instance, emasculates the art of Shakespeare or Congreve by removing one or two scenes which all nice people admit to be nasty, these arrogant tourists, just back from a trip to eternity, make bold to call him not only hard but filthy names. To anyone used to the pleasures of the world of absolute values – the pleasures of Shakespeare and Congreve are of that world naturally – the pleasures of below-stairs are much of muchness. He cannot bother to distinguish the tattle of the servants-hall from the rattle of the scullery. Wherefore, to such a one, obliged by sickness perhaps or lassitude to spend an evening here below, it will not greatly signify whether that evening be lost at a bar or at *The Miracle*, in a brothel or reading one of the late Mr Galsworthy's novels.'*

Unfortunately, most Shakespeare-criticism from the earliest times to the present day has been undertaken by the 'cultured' – the critics and the academics – who dislike and misunderstand the real nature of Shakespeare's art almost as much as the public which, if it has studied the Bard at school or university, goes occasionally to a perform-

---

* *Enjoying Pictures* by Clive Bell (1934). This book is not as well known as it should be. I am under the impression it was withdrawn owing to a threatened libel-action.

ance as a duty or, if it has not, sedulously avoids contamina-
tion. The fact that the actor's profession, since Irving betrayed it by accepting a knighthood, has become socially
respectable (though roguery and vagabondage lie nearer
the surface, waiting to erupt, than the stalls think) makes for
a certain factitious popularity of certain selected Shake-
speariana among the Philistines and, one feels, if it could only
be proved beyond doubt that the plays were written by the
Earl of Oxford or even by Francis Bacon (who was only a
Viscount) they might become very popular indeed. But
even those who perforce accept 'the man from Stratford'
boggle at the idea of the actor-playwright of the Globe. It is
too disturbing to accepted values.

He is fully recognisable, perhaps, only to those of his own
profession. In this sense he remains the 'our' Shakespeare
of Heminges and Condell and, though it is an exaggeration,
it may point the way to the truth to say than an actor who
has played in little but pantomime in Blackpool has more
natural and intuitive understanding of Shakespeare than the
most learned professor.

Even when it is realised that Shakespeare cannot be
divorced from the stage, there is often an attempt to mini-
mise the meaning of it. Mr Halliday, for example, in the
latest life of Shakespeare, writes: 'It seems to me that too
much emphasis has been placed on Shakespeare as an
actor. Although he probably began his London career as a
player, although nobody knew more about acting and stage-
craft than he, by the time he was a full adventurer with the
Chamberlain's with half a dozen plays to his credit, his
fellows must have realised that he was far too valuable an
asset to be wasted on the memorising of long parts and un-
profitable travel in the provinces; it would be only common
sense therefore to reduce his acting to the playing of minor
parts and to leave him free to write plays for them while
they went on their summer tours.'

This not only shows a misunderstanding of the nature

of the theatre then or now, but it illustrates admirably the process of restoring 'respectability' to Shakespeare. He went home to New Place and, ensconced in that ivory tower, penned his masterpieces, like some modern author retiring to his place in the country to write next year's best-seller. What could be more acceptable to English public opinion which, as Wilde has reminded us, 'is an attempt to organise the ignorance of the community and to elevate it to the dignity of physical force?' Here is a comprehensible 'artist' confined within the limits of gossip-column accepti-bility. The facts, however, are a little more complicated than that.

Both tradition and the customs of the time suggest that Shakespeare's first connection with his Company was as prompter's boy or attendant. The prompter was also the 'book-keeper,' that is to say, it was his responsibility to see that a fair copy of the play in hand was submitted for censor-ship to the Lord Chamberlain, that the cuts made were observed and that any additional matter inserted during rehearsals was duly entered on the copy. But he was also the 'stage-keeper' who had to ensure that all the stage properties were in their places. In his triple office, he was indeed a 'Jack of all work,' a *Johannes factotum*, and in the person of Quince in *A Midsummer Night's Dream* Shakespeare has left a sketch of him. As that play was written just about the time Shakespeare became a full member of the company, Baldwin suggests that 'it may be regarded as his graduating exercise, in which with gentle satire he pays his respects to his former position.'

During his years of apprenticeship as book-keeper – prompter – stage-keeper, Shakespeare seems to have had the additional personal responsibility of rehashing the old plays the company decided to put on. The early playwrights of the company were Marlowe, Kyd and Greene. As 'book-keeper,' Shakespeare could study their work at close quarters; as 'prompter,' he would become familiar with their lines;

as 'play-patcher' he might add to or alter them.* Thus, hack-wise, he proceeded to authorship. He seems to have plagiarised a reasonable amount (though the modern connotation of the world does not, perhaps, quite convey the ordinariness of the action in the circumstances) and to have been very sure of himself.

A man of the theatre today will immediately recognise him – the stage-struck provincial in his 'twenties, getting into the theatre somehow and unswerving in his devotion to it; doing his turn as ASM; 'on the book' at rehearsals; determined to write plays for himself and carefully imitating the current fashion, modelling himself on his masters,† but for the moment more concerned with his poetry, which he eventually induces a former schoolfellow of his to publish and dedicates to the aristocratic leader of the 'younger set,' who has also become his friend. 'Sweet Mr Shakespeare' he may have been to some, but his elders might be forgiven for resenting both his arrogance and his good-fortune; and the University-educated writers – Greene and Marlowe were both Cambridge men – were not altogether wrong in regarding him as a portent of an unwelcome shape of things to come.

One remembers Greene now largely because his waspish death-bed protest in 1592 is the first known reference to Shakespeare's theatrical career, and is valuable for 'dating' plays. Because it criticises 'the Bard' it is held, in a curious 'literary' way, to redound to Greene's discredit. But, in its context, it is comprehensible enough. Greene was a pioneer in the theatre – his 'Friar Bacon and Friar Bungay' is still occasionally acted – a poet and a writer with thirty-eight publications of various sorts to his name. He was thirty-two and had been responsible for the original versions of the

---

* It is difficult to realise, now that these plays have become 'classics,' how anonymous were the 'scripts' at the time. No one knows who wrote *Arden of Feversham*; it is only by inference that *Tamburlaine* is credited to Marlowe and by accident that we know *The Spanish Tragedy* to be Kyd's.

† *Richard III* is his eventual exercise in the style of Marlowe: *Titus Andronicus* in that of Kyd.

Henry VI plays which Shakespeare had 'worked over' and for which that intolerable newcomer (only four years his junior) was now taking the credit. Warning his friends against the new acting companies, Greene wrote: 'Trust them not; for there is an upstart crow, beautified with our feathers, that with his 'Tiger's heart wrapt in a Player's hide,'* supposes he is as well able to bombast out a blank verse as the best of you: and being an absolute *Johannes factotum* is, in his own conceit, the only Shake-scene in a country.'

It is, as I said, comprehensible enough. What is more to the point, it is, to those who look at 'our Shakespeare' with theatrically experienced eyes, recognisable enough.

When Shakespeare became more experienced as a dramatist and served the company in that capacity, he had to provide them, according to the custom of the time, with two plays a year. Reference has already been made to the interaction between the playwright and actor but, because the theatrical reality is so different from the romantic picture of a dramatist writing from his imagination *in vacuo* and 'hoping some manager will be interested and put the play on,' it is worth quoting Baldwin's epitome of the conditions: 'Shakespeare's play was to be produced not by some company, but by the particular company to which he belonged. Each part was to be taken, not by some actor to be picked from the world's supply, but by a specific actor already in the company, Richard Burbage or John Heminges, etc. Nor was his problem lessened by the fact that in all this he was not the master but the servant. He did not pick the company either directly or indirectly, but the company picked him. The company was not fitted to the play, but the play to the company. This situation had its effect on every stage of the play . . . At every stage the author's work was subject to direction and suggestion from the company. Since the company was paying good money to have the play con-

---

* A reference to the description of Queen Margaret 'O tiger's heart wrapped in a woman's hide' in 3 *Henry VI* I. iv. 137.

structed, it took proper precautions to see that the play was
to its liking.'

These were the practical conditions under which Shakespeare had to write, this the rigid mould into which the
'inspiration' was poured. And rising out of the internal
were external limitations. Topical popularity was as necessary
for success then as now. The theatre, more than most arts, is
a thing of the moment – the one place where it is impossible
consciously to 'write for posterity.' Paradoxically, Shakespeare's supreme masterpiece, *Macbeth*, is of all the plays
the most obviously topical, constructed to please the new
King, whose interest in witches was one ruling passion and
whose delight in hunting another. The witches are obvious
enough, as is the vision of the union of the Crowns; but
today many may overlook that Macbeth's speech to the
murderers pays discreet tribute to James's interest in dogs:

> Ay, in the catalogue ye go for men;
> As hounds and greyhounds, mongrels, spaniels, curs,
> Shoughs, water-rugs, and demi-wolves are clept
> All by the name of dogs: the valued file
> Distinguishes the swift, the slow, the subtle,
> The housekeeper, the hunter, every one
> According to the gift which bounteous nature
> Hath in him closed.

Shakespeare's accommodation to the needs of the company
brought him his measure of financial success and he used
his money as one would have expected an actor to use it.
He invested it in property. The motives behind his purchases
may not, as I have suggested earlier, have been dictated
by simple acquisitiveness. Nor, if the story is true which
his godson Davenant told – that Southampton once gave
Shakespeare a thousand pounds* – could he ever have been

* Modern critics have discounted the story on the grounds of the
vastness of the sum – about £60,000 in modern currency. Considering
Southampton's enormous wealth and his relationship with Shakespeare,
it seems, however, quite in character.

in great need of money. But the uncertainties of an actor's life, accentuated by the ephemeral nature of theatrical popularity, seem to have made through the ages 'real estate' a poor player's goal. And Shakespeare was no exception. As Ivor Brown has it, 'Antony might hurl away an empire; his creator went out and bought another acre.'

It has been held against him in some quarters. Because nearly all the manuscripts relating to him which have survived are legal documents about property, he appears as an 'acquisitive bourgeois.' And it must be admitted that the picture that emerges of a keen business man, willing to lend but almost as adamant as Shylock about repayment, buying up the Stratford corn-supply in a period of bad harvests, investing in 'knit-stockings' which were selling very well at Evesham, in addition to the various property deals, is not particularly pleasant. 'But you, gods, give us some faults to make us men.'

Yet it was surely not parsimony which made him reluctant to attend parties. There are even men of theatre today who refuse that routine on the grounds that they have better use for their time. 'He was not a company keeper: lived in Shoreditch: would not be debauched, and, if invited to, writ; he was in pain.' That brief sentence from Aubrey's *Brief Life* of him is necessary to complete the portrait of 'our Shakespeare.'

XIV : Angry Apes

THE death-bed at Stratford dwarfs, in retrospect, everything else that happened in England on St George's
Day, 1616. We see it now as the earthly end of the greatest
of Englishmen. Frank Harris's famous sentence, written
half a century ago, remains as true as ever: 'In a dull half-
conscious way, the English are beginning to realise that the
biggest thing they have done in the world yet is to produce
Shakespeare.'

But it was very far from being seen so at the time, and as,
in any age, the nature of greatness is seldom understood
and the process of honouring yesterday's prophets while
stoning today's is wearyingly repetitive, it is seldom seen
as it was even now. 'The Bard' is made in the image of his
worshippers.

The kind of 'greatness' that is easily understood is, at all
times, that associated with rank and power – the outward
forms which embody, almost by definition, the reverse of true
greatness. It is *Measure for Measure* again:

> Man, proud man,
> Dress'd in a little brief authority
> . . . like an angry ape
> Plays such fantastic tricks before high heaven
> As make the angels weep.

By one of the curious coincidences of history, the day
Shakespeare died witnessed also certain moments in the lives
of the great of the land. George Villiers, a youth of twenty-

three, of boundless ambition and some beauty, had captivated the king. He eventually became, as first Duke of
Buckingham, the most disastrous royal minion in our
history. At the beginning of that April, he had been 'nearly
mad' because of a threatened attack of smallpox which,
had it left its marks, 'would have ended his favour.' In his
relations with King James he was at that critical period when
he could have held him neither by the promise of delight with-
held nor by the bond of long-shared friendship. To have lost
his looks at that point would have been to lose everything. But
the danger passed. His influence became so great 'as what
he will shall be.' And the King celebrated the occasion by
awarding him, on that 23 April 1616, the highest honour of
chivalry – the Order of the Garter.

A month earlier, Sir Walter Raleigh had been released
from his twelve years of captivity in the Tower and given
permission to assemble a fleet to go to Guiana in search of
gold for the King and his catamite. Nearly everyone but
Raleigh himself realised that the expedition would be –
as it was – his death-warrant. Just before James came up to
London from Theobalds 'to celebrate St George's Feast,'
the Spanish Ambassador had an audience with him, discovered what was afoot and took steps to meet it. In his
letter sent to the King of Spain by the next post he asked
leave to visit Madrid to speak personally to him about 'the
formation of another company for Guiana, the prime
promoter and originator of which is Sir Walter Raleigh.'
Thus, while Raleigh himself, sanguine as ever, was collecting
men and ships, his ultimate doom was sealed.

So Raleigh comes into the pattern of the day, giving a
further dimension to it. For one thing, Raleigh had real
greatness, in that he too was a poet, and though, as the leader
of the anti-Essex faction, he was Shakespeare's butt in
Love's Labour's Lost, he was, of all the power-crazed courtiers
in the closing years of Queen Elizabeth I's reign, the only
one worth posterity's attention. Twelve years older than

Shakespeare, he was, when Shakespeare arrived in London, the Queen's paramour, calling attention to the fact by his seal, showing the famous cloak by which he first won her favour, and his motto, *Amore et Virtute.** He was soon to fall from power before the onslaught of young Essex on the Queen's ageing sexuality, but he had had his moment of power and magnificence and the declension from Raleigh, as the bedchamber power behind the English throne, to Villiers, who now occupied that place, was a measure of the gradual decadence in high places during Shakespeare's lifetime.

There is one more facet to the day. As Shakespeare lay dying, Oliver Cromwell, within two days of his sixteenth birthday, was admitted to Sidney Sussex College, Cambridge. '*Oliverius Cromwell Huntingdoniensis,*' runs the register, '*admissum ad commeatum Sociorum Aprilis vicesimo tertio.*' Oliver was to rule, not as Raleigh and Villiers had ruled, but of himself by the power within himself. Here was greatness of another order.

Cromwell represented, in his triumphant Puritanism, the defeat of all that Shakespeare stood for. Under his rule the theatres were closed. An affirmative answer was given to the *Twelfth Night* question: 'Dost thou think, because thou art virtuous, there shall be no more cakes and ale?' But the triumph was temporary only. In the world of affairs, it was necessary for Cromwell to redress the balance of Villiers, for true power to set to rights a little the havoc wrought by false. Yet as the brawl of the Civil War and the killing of the King had nothing to do with the world of Shakespeare's greatness (which was more truly represented by those who absented themselves from Naseby and got on with the haymaking), his values surged back the more strongly. And it is not without interest that, on the one occasion under the

* This seal forms one of the illustrations to Walter Oakeshott's *The Queen and the Poet* (1960) and is an additional confirmation of the traditional story.

Protectorate when Cromwell relaxed the rule it was in favour of Davenant, who was permitted in the May of 1656 to present an Italian opera *An Entertainment at Rutland House* in Charterhouse Yard.

So the great who share that St George's Day with the actor-playwright – a Queen's favourite, a King's minion and a military dictator – are but the background for his greatness. What that greatness was is best epitomised in a sentence of Goethe's: 'I have often said and I will often repeat that the final cause and consummation of all natural and human activity is dramatic poetry.' Shakespeare took it to its furthest reach and beside his creations those other 'great' have become as shadows. Hamlet has had more influence on the world than Oliver Cromwell, great though he was.

Raleigh, great too in his own right, explained in his last speech on the scaffold: 'I have been a seafaring man, a soldier and a courtier, and in the temptations of the least of these, there is enough to overthrow a good mind and a good man.' But he was also a poet, an historian and a philosopher and, though in the accidents of life he stood against Shakespeare, in the realm of final values he is not altogether unworthy to stand with him.

XV: Don Armado

In 1587, when Shakespeare was beginning his career in the lowliest position in the theatre, Raleigh had been Queen Elizabeth I's lover for about five years. At thirty-five, he was Member of Parliament for Devonshire, Lord Warden of the Stanneries, Lieutenant of the County of Cornwall and Vice-Admiral of Devon and Cornwall. His London residence was Durham House in the Strand, where he kept 'forty men and horses' as his personal bodyguard. He was Captain of the Queen's Guard, the most coveted of posts because it kept the occupant of it always near the Queen, with the right of access to her at all times. He was also 'the best hated man in the world, in Court, city and country' – and one of the most remarkable. Six feet tall, with a swarthy complexion, long, melancholy face, pointed beard and heavily-lidded eyes, he outdistanced every fashion. His jewelled shoes were said to be worth more than 6,600 gold pieces; his hat-band of pearls, his ear-rings, the silks and damasks he wore and the ornaments with which he bedecked himself were worth a king's ransom. In his Devonshire accent (which always amused Elizabeth and which he kept all his life), he uttered witticisms which wounded and insults which none dared challenge.

The ballad-makers sang:

> Raleigh doth time bestride
> He sits 'twixt wind and tide,
> Yet uphill he cannot ride
> For all his bloody pride . . .

There seemed, however, nothing to prevent him riding as high as he wished until, that year, the young Earl of Essex came to Court. Essex was the Queen's cousin, Leicester's step-son, the elder Cecil's ward. He had a handsome presence, a personality that could sway crowds as well as individuals, and some of the oldest blood in England. His ancestry could be traced back directly to Edward III, but he was descended also from most of the great mediaeval houses which had intermarried with the Plantagenets. He might be the poorest earl in England, but he was among the most certain aristocrats. At twenty he spoke to the Queen, as if by right, in tones which Raleigh, the obscure Devonshire gentleman, would never dare use, for all his pride of place. The summer was spent in bitter bickerings between them. Essex took advantage of Raleigh's enforced immobility as Captain of the Guard to ask the Queen, in his hearing: 'What comfort can I have to give myself over to a mistress that is in awe of such a man?' Elizabeth did all she could to drive the two into friendship ('which rather,' as Essex remarked, 'shall drive me to many other extremities') and Raleigh remained the official favourite. But his days were numbered. Though Essex temporarily fell from what favour he had by marrying Sir Philip Sidney's widow, Raleigh fell further and finally by himself marrying one of Elizabeth's maids-of-honour secretly early in 1592.

The Queen's fury knew no bounds. She had been sufficiently angry about Essex's marriage, though it was in one sense proper enough for a young nobleman to give his house an heir. But for Raleigh, apparently a confirmed bachelor at forty, dependent on her for all he had, to make a very ordinary marriage suggested only one explaination, which was, in fact, the true one – that he had fallen in love with the woman he made his wife. Elizabeth sent them both to the Tower and when they were released banished them from Court for five years. So Raleigh retired to the country estate, Sherborne Castle in Dorset, which the Queen had given

him not long before he married, and this became from the
end of 1592 the centre of that intellectual ferment known as
'the School of Night.'

The 'School of Night' might be described in modern terms
as a cross between a club and a learned society. Its members
were friends bound together by their intellectual interests.
The outstanding personality of the school was Thomas
Harriot, who was Raleigh's closest friend throughout his
life and was with him the night before his execution. He
was one of the greatest scientists of the time. He was ahead
of Galileo in his use of the telescope by which he used
'especially to see Venus horned like the Moon and the spots
in the Sun,' and he made a precise observation of Halley's
Comet in 1609. As a mathematician, his discoveries in
algebra and pure mathematics were far in advance of his
age, though, as he refused to publish during his lifetime,
others gained credit for his discoveries.

Sharing Harriot's interests were two eccentric noblemen,
the thirty-year-old Earl of Northumberland, whose scientific
experiments earned him the nickname of 'the Wizard Earl'
and the thirty-four-year-old Earl of Derby, poet, alchemist
and suspected witch, who died suddenly under circumstances
which suggested poison in 1594.

On the literary side, Raleigh was its poet – and Spenser
when he was in England; Marlowe was its dramatist
(Raleigh served him as a model for certain aspects of Dr
Faustus) and George Chapman, a strange, retiring figure,
more interested in mysticism than in mathematics, became
its chief playwright after Marlowe's murder in the May of
1593. When Marlowe died in a tavern brawl just as the
Privy Council was preparing to arrest him on the charges
of blasphemy and atheism, Raleigh (against whom the
public was prepared to believe anything) was suspected of
having a hand in his death to prevent any revelations he
might make under torture about the 'School of Night,' and a
Commission on Atheism was set up at Cerne Abbas, not

far from Sherborne, to investigate the attitude of Marlowe, Raleigh and others to conventional beliefs.

They were worth investigating. 'The School of Night' questioned everything, from the structure of the Bible to the structure of the Universe and it brought together in its studies the various trends of thought which made the age such a ferment of excitement. The astronomical discoveries of Harriot, combined with the geographical explorations of Raleigh had shattered the old comfortable view of the world. The examination of the Bible led them to speculate as to whether there might have been 'men before Adam' and to notice certain contradictions in the Old Testament narratives–'contrarieties of Scripture' as Marlowe called them. And the new political philosophy of Machiavelli, with its ruthless analysis of the realities of power, clarified the motives of men governing. Harriot became in popular estimation 'that devil' and with him, in necromancy, were classed Northumberland and Derby: Marlowe was a blasphemous atheist, whose violent death was a judgment from Heaven; Raleigh was, as well as an atheist, indistinguishable from that

> Damnable fiend of Hell
> Mischievous Machiavel.

The figure of Machiavelli haunted the Elizabethans and Elizabethan drama has been defined in terms of it as 'the terror-stricken meeting of the England of Elizabeth with the Italy of the late Renaissance.' On the stage, the master-Machiavel was to be Shakespeare's Iago; in popular estimation in real life it was Sir Walter Raleigh.

The Commission on Atheism at Cerne Abbas came to nothing, but another attack on the School was more lasting, for *Love's Labour's Lost* was, among other things, Shakespeare's account of 'the School of Night.' Shakespeare was, at this moment, as passionately attached to Southampton (*Venus and Adonis* was published in 1593) as Southampton was to Essex, and the manifesto had a political as well as a personal motive.

As long ago as 1923 Sir Arthur Quiller-Couch and
Professor Dover Wilson, in their preface to their edition of
Love's Labour's Lost drew attention to the topicality of the
play in 1593. They pointed out that for that year we have
the following data: 'A favourite, Raleigh, suddenly fallen
from power, and his friends discredited by rumours of their
trafficking with Copernican astronomics and atheism; a
rival party – that of Essex – to which Shakespeare was
vowed, in suit of his young patron, the Earl of Southampton,
Essex's devoted friend; a Christmas of 1593 during which the
theatres were shut by reason of the plague; a play, obviously
topical, designed for a polite audience, abounding in shrewd
hits at certain devotees of a "School of Night," presented as
fantastics.'

The theory, since then, has been elaborated* and attacked,
and recently triumphantly vindicated by Walter Oakeshott
in *The Queen and the Poet*.

The young Shakespeare, in the circumstances, was at
pains to make his picture of Raleigh as wounding as he
could. He starts with the supreme insult of representing him
as a Spaniard, Don Armado, but he leaves no doubt in
the minds of any of the audience who is intended by the
knight who spends his time writing poetry, who addresses
his servant with a West Country 'Chirrah,' who is noted for
the magnificence of his dress and his tales of travel, who is
short of money and whose 'humour is lofty, his discourse
peremptory, his tongue filed, his eye ambitious, his gait
majestical and his general behaviour vain, ridiculous and
thrasonical.' To underline the identity, if it were necessary,
he introduces the rhyme:

> The Fox, the Ape and the Humble Bee
> Were still at odds, being but three . . .
> Until the Goose came out of door
> Staying the odds by adding four.

* Especially in M. C. Bradbrook's brilliant *The School of Night* (1936).

– the goose being Elizabeth Throckmorton, whom Raleigh married, and the other three animals representing aspects of Raleigh himself, the Fox his Machiavellianism; the Ape his flattery and the Humble Bee his buzzing about the Court. He points it still further in one couplet in which he epitomises Raleigh's dark complexion, his atheism, his recent imprisonment and his School:

> O paradox! Black is the badge of Hell,
> The hue of dungeons and the School of Night.

As Dr Oakeshott has put it: 'The first audience who came to see the play knew before it began that Raleigh, in the blackest disgrace, was one of the objects of its mockery. When Armado was first mentioned:

> A man in all the world's new fashion planted
> That hath a mint of phrases in his brain:
> One who the music of his own vain tongue
> Doth ravish like enchanting harmony:
> A man of complement whom right and wrong
> Have chose as umpire of their mutiny

they recognised the real Raleigh rather than the play's Armado.'

Yet, paradoxically, it was the real Raleigh, past his fortieth birthday and having experienced the realities of power, whom the real Shakespeare, not yet at his thirtieth and without any experience except the fringe of Southampton House, might have saluted in very different terms.

In prison, he had just written his great poem, *The Lie*, in which he imagines himself at the point of death, sending his soul to give his last message to the world:

> Say to the Court, it glows
>   And shines like rotten wood;
> Say to the Church it shows
>   What's good and doth no good.
>   If Church and Court reply,
>   Then give them both the lie.

> Tell potentates they live
>   Acting by others' action;
> Not loved unless they give,
>   Not strong but by a faction.
>   If potentates reply
>   Give potentates the lie
>
> Tell men of high condition,
>   That manage the Estate,
> Their purpose is ambition,
>   Their practice only hate;
>   And if they once reply,
>   Then give them all the lie . . .

This was but an epitome of Shakespeare's own attitude ten years later when experience had taught him a little; and it was a poem which is likely to last as long as his own. Yet, gaily partisan, he used its popularity merely for a topical laugh in *Love's Labour's Lost* when the King says of Armado, 'I love to hear him lie,' just as he refers to Raleigh's long and superb *Cynthia* poem in Armado's: 'Assist me, some extemporal god of rhyme, for I am sure I shall turn sonnet . . . Devise wit, write pen, for I am for whole volumes in folio.'

Political partnership was, indeed, to increase the rift; for it was Raleigh who, as Captain of the Guard and back in favour, broke Essex. When, at Essex's trial, Raleigh took the oath, Essex called out: 'What booteth it to swear the fox?' and suggested that a folio would be more appropriate than a small Bible. Yet when he came on the scaffold, Essex admitted that Raleigh was a true servant to Queen and State and, in his last moments, asked for him. But Raleigh was not by the block. Though he had at first, as Captain of the Guard, taken up his position there, the murmuring of spectators, who interpreted the action as a gloating over a rival's death, had caused him to withdraw to the armoury, from the window of which he watched the final act. When it was over, men noticed that his face was bitter with gloom.

On the accession of James I, the wheel of fortune turned once more. To the King, Essex was 'my martyr' and Raleigh, eventually 'framed' for a plot of which he was entirely innocent, was sent to the Tower. He remained there for twelve years, and was released just before Shakespeare's death. In prison he wrote his great *History of the World*, which appeared in 1614 and whose underlying philosophy is not very different from Shakespeare's. Raleigh sees history as the dealings of God with individuals: 'God, whom the wisest men acknowledge to be a power ineffable and virtue infinite: a light by abundant clarity invisible: an understanding which only itself can comprehend; an essence eternal and spiritual, of absolute pureness and simplicity, was and is pleased to make Himself known by the work of the world' – thus it opens. What is interesting is the spectacle of individual destinies, for Nature delights in apparent variety. 'Change of fortune in the great theatre is but as change of garments in the less, for when on the one or the other every man wears but his own skin the players are all alike.'

Only at death do men understand reality. 'It is therefore Death alone that can suddenly make man to know himself. He tells the proud and insolent that they were but abjects, and humbles them at the instant, makes them cry, complain, repent, yea, even to hate their fore-passed happiness. He takes account of the rich and proves him a beggar, a naked beggar, which hath interest in nothing but the gravel that fills his mouth. He holds a glass before the eyes of the most beautiful and makes them see therein their deformity and rottenness: and they acknowledge it.' This passage leads to the famous apostrophe to Death, which has been rightly called the most perfect prose in the English language: 'O eloquent, just and mighty Death! Whom none could advise, thou hast persuaded; what none hath dared, thou hast done;

and whom all the world hath flattered, thou only hast cast
out of the world and despised; thou hast drawn together all
the far-stretched greatness, all the pride, cruelty and
ambition of man and covered it over with these two narrow
words, *Hic Jacet*.'

With such a philosophy as the foundation of the structure
of his history, Raleigh drew on his experience of statecraft
to elucidate and, with some cynicism, to enunciate the truth
that contemporary history is in any age impossible: 'I know
it will be said by many that I might have been more pleasing
if I had written the story of mine own times, having been
permitted to draw water as near the well-head as another.
To this I answer that whosoever in writing a modern history
shall follow Truth too near the heels, it may haply strike out
his teeth.'

Some of the judgments he made, in passing, in the preface
more than justified him. His reference to Henry VIII was
even more deadly than Shakespeare's: 'If all the pictures
and patterns of merciless princes were lost in the world,
they might all again be painted to the life out of the story
of this King.' It was this which caused King James to order
the suppression of the book, on the ground that the author
was 'too saucy in censoring princes.'

In 1613, Raleigh engaged Ben Jonson as tutor to his
unsatisfactory son, Wat. By this time Jonson and Shakespeare had experienced fifteen years of friendship and rivalry.
In 1598, Shakespeare had acted in Jonson's play *Every Man
in his Humour* and, according to tradition, had been instru-
mental in getting his company to perform it. Thus Shakespeare's acquaintance with Ben Jonson, who was twelve
years his junior, 'began with a remarkable piece of humanity
and good nature. Mr Jonson, who was at that time altogether
unknown to the world, had offered one of his plays to the
players in order to have it acted, and the persons into whose
hands it was put, after having turned it carelessly and
superciliously over, were just upon returning it to him with

an ill-natured answer that it would be of no service to their company when Shakespeare luckily cast his eye upon it and found something so well in it as to engage him first to read it through and afterwards to recommend Mr Jonson and his writing to the public. After this they were professed friends.' Shakespeare's name stands first in the list of players and it is possible that he played the elder Knowell.

Jonson, the scholar, the constructor of plays on classical models, the taker of infinite pains, paid notable enough tributes to Shakespeare though both during his life and after his death he indulged in inevitable acidities. It was Jonson who said that Shakespeare 'wanted art' and first drew attention to the fact that 'Shakespeare in a play brought in a number of men saying they had suffered shipwreck in Bohemia, where there is no sea near by a hundred miles'; who when told that Shakespeare 'never blotted a line' retorted 'Would he had blotted a thousand' and remarked acidly that he 'flowed with that facility that sometimes it was necessary he should be stopped'; who, even in his panegyric, could not resist repeating that Shakespeare had 'small Latin and less Greek.' Shakespeare's traditional retort to this is said to have occurred when he stood godfather to one of Jonson's children. After the christening, Ben asked him why he was looking so serious. 'No, faith, Ben,' says he: 'not I, but I have been considering a great while what should be the fittest gift for me to bestow upon my god-child and I have resolved at last.' 'I prithee, what?' says he. 'I' faith, Ben, I'll e'en give him a dozen good Lattin spoons* and thou shalt translate them.'

According to Fuller, 'many were the wit combats between Shakespeare and Ben Jonson, which two I behold like a Spanish great galleon and an English man-of-war; Master Jonson (like the former) was built far higher in learning, solid, but slow in his performances. Shakespeare, with the English man-of-war, lesser in bulk, but lighter in sailing,

* Lattin is a mixed metal resembling brass.

could turn with all tides, tack about and take advantage of all winds, by the quickness of his wit and invention.'

Jonson, passionate and quarrelsome, 'jealous of every word and action of those about him (especially after drink, which is one of the elements in which he liveth),' killed a fellow-actor in a duel a few days after the production of *Every Man in his Humour* and for it was branded on the thumb and imprisoned. In prison, he became a Catholic and remained one for twelve years, consorting openly with the 'Gunpowder Plot' conspirators and, in 1606, was reported as a recusant, with the additional charge: 'He is a poet and is by fame a seducer of youth to the Popish religion.' Under pressure, he conformed again in 1610 and in token of it 'drank out all the full cup of wine' at the Communion service. Thereafter, in argument at least, he was 'for any religion, being versed in both.'

It was as a returned Protestant that he offered his services to Sir Walter Raleigh and, according to his own account, wrote 'a piece to him of the Punic War which he altered and set in his book' for 'the best wits of England were employed for making of his *History*.' Ben's visit to Paris in charge of Raleigh's son was not altogether successful, because 'this youth, being knavishly inclined . . . caused him to be drunken and dead drunk, so that he knew not where he was. Thereafter he laid him on a car which he made to be drawn by pioneers through the streets, at every corner showing his governor stretched out and telling them that was a more lively image of the Crucifix than any they had.' Raleigh, when he heard of it, 'abhorred it' and, as far as is known, any connection between Raleigh and Ben Jonson ceased.

Raleigh was released from the Tower, a month before Shakespeare died, after paying £750 apiece to Villiers's brother and half-brother. He received from the Privy Council a letter: 'His Majesty, out of his gracious inclination towards you, being pleased to release you out of your imprisonment in the Tower, to go abroad with a keeper, to make your provisions for your intended voyage, we think it good to admonish you . . . that you should not presume to resort wither to His Majesty's Court, the Queen's or the Prince's; nor go into any public assemblies whatsoever . . . but only that you are to use the benefit of His Majesty's grace to follow the business which you are to undertake and for which, upon your humble request, His Majesty hath graciously pleased to grant you that freedom.'

Thus it was that on St George's Day, 1616, Sir Walter Raleigh was arranging for the building of his new ship, the *Destiny*, in which he was to sail on his last fruitless quest for gold, and the Spanish Ambassador, who was to have his head in the end, was raging at the King for the enlargement of 'that old pirate, bred under the English virago, and by her fleshed in Spanish blood and ruin.'

XVI : Steenie

Raleigh's release from the Tower came sooner than was intended because his 'lodgings' there were needed for the Earl and Countess of Somerset.

It was in 1607 – the year of *Timon of Athens* – that the Earl, then plain Robert Kerr, came into favour; and his ascendancy over the King outlasted Shakespeare's working life. Kerr, 'rather well compacted than tall; his features and favour comely and handsome rather than beautiful,' had for a short time been one of James's pages in Scotland; but failed to make a decisive impact on the King till, in London in 1607 in a tilting match on the anniversary of the coronation, he was thrown from his horse and broke his arm. The King immediately lost all interest in the remainder of the jousting, ordered it to be finished as soon as possible, and hurried to the house near Charing Cross where Kerr had been taken. Thereafter there were daily visits. The implication was clear to the Court. 'Lord!' wrote an observer, 'how the great men flocked there to see him and to offer to his Shrine in such abundance that the King was forced to lay a restraint, lest it might retard his recovery.'

The King, keeping Kerr to himself, decided to mould him into a perfect companion. He taught him Latin every morning – though as one ungenerous observer remarked, someone ought to have taught him English 'for he is a Scotch lad and hath much need of better language'; he instructed him in statecraft and encouraged him to instruct himself in 'art and device.' Kerr 'changed his tailors and

155

tiremen many times and all to please the prince.' James
knighted him and, in the years that followed, created him
Viscount Rochester and Earl of Somerset; made him, on
Cecil's death in 1612, private secretary with the patronage
of all the offices of State in his hands, and later Lord Treasurer
of Scotland, Lord Privy Seal and Lord Chamberlain.

One of James's first considerations for the new favourite
was to find an estate for him, and when Cecil suggested
giving him Raleigh's manor of Sherborne, the King wrote
gratefully: 'The more I think of your remembrance of
Robert Kerr for yon manor of Sherborne, the more cause I
have to conclude that your mind ever watcheth to seek out
all advantages for my honour and contentment.' Consequently at the end of 1607 the Crown commenced proceedings to invalidate Raleigh's title to his home. In the January
of 1608, Raleigh wrote from the Tower to Kerr: 'Sir, After
many great losses and many years' sorrow it has come to my
knowledge that yourself (whom I know not but by an
honourable fame) have been persuaded to give me and mine
our last fatal blow, by obtaining from His Majesty the
inheritance of my children and nephews, lost in law for want
of words . . . Sir, seeing your day is but now in the dawn
and mine come to the evening – your own virtues and the
King's grace assuring you of many good fortunes and much
honour – I beseech you not to begin your first buildings on
the ruin of the innocent; and that their griefs and sorrows
do not attend your first plantation . . .'

Kerr did not answer the letter. Lady Raleigh went to
plead in person to James who, at first ignoring her, finally
muttered: 'I mun have the land. I mun have it for Kerr.'
The Courts naturally found for the Crown and a letter-
writer that January noted: 'Sir Walter Raleigh's estate is
fallen into the King's hands by reason of a flaw in the conveyance. He hath bestowed it on Sir Robert Kerr.' But at
this point, Henry, Prince of Wales, who was Raleigh's
friend, who had said contemptuously: 'No one but my

father would keep such a bird in a cage,' and for whom
Raleigh was writing his *History of the World*, went angrily
to the King and demanded Sherborne for himself. James
gave way and bought Kerr off with £25,000 (in the currency
of the time).

It was not long before the inevitable hatred of the King's
son for the King's minion flared into open hostility. Popular
rumour (not without foundation) linked the Prince's
name with that of the dissolute young Countess of Essex,
Frances Howard, who was also desired by Kerr. With her
to add fuel to the flames, all the King's efforts at reconcilia-
tion were useless. When Kerr was narrowly prevented from
hitting the Prince over the head with a tennis-racket, the
scandal was sufficiently public, but Henry added to it by his
remark, when someone brought him one of the lady's gloves,
that 'he scorned it since it had been stretched by another.'

In the autumn of 1612, Henry fell ill of what was probably
typhoid, and in spite of all the efforts of his physicians –
including a last-minute prescription made by Raleigh in
the Tower – he died. The country was swept by a genuine
sorrow and a no less genuine suspicion. It was said that Kerr,
the Howards and even James himself had poisoned the
Prince.

Cecil also died that year. There were many epitaphs on
him, among them one from Raleigh. It is unprintable, as most
of them are. Of the remainder, the simplest and most apt
was:

> Here lies Robin Crookback; unjustly reckoned
> A Richard the Third, he was Judas the Second.

With his death and that of Prince Henry, the whole
political situation changed. As long as Cecil lived and ruled
and as long as the Prince, under Raleigh's tutelage, headed
the anti-Spanish party, the main lines of James's policy
followed those of Elizabeth I and the influence of the
minion of the moment was personal only. But with Charles

(later Charles I), a sickly boy of twelve, as Prince of Wales and with no one stronger than Pembroke to lead the anti-Spanish group, the Favouriteship assumed quite another aspect. The pro-Spanish Howards determined to make a bid for the control of the King through Kerr, with Frances Howard as the bait.

The death of Prince Henry had removed the rival lover, but the husband remained an insuperable barrier. It was therefore decided that the Countess must be divorced and unofficial conversations on the subject were begun early in 1613, though nothing serious could be done until the conclusion of the dynastic marriage between Princess Elizabeth, the King's daughter, and the Elector Palatine, which was celebrated on St Valentine's Day at the expense (including the festivities) of £93,278 – in the currency of the time – to the depleted exchequer. It is possible that *Henry VIII*, which was performed later in the year, was intended for this occasion, since the Princess was named after Queen Elizabeth I, with whose birth the play ends; but the plays of Shakespeare's actually given as part of the wedding festivities were *The Tempest*, *Much Ado about Nothing*, *Othello* and *The Winter's Tale* and, possibly, *The Merry Wives of Windsor* and *Julius Caesar*.*

The Princess and her husband did not leave England till late in April and the usual Accession Day tournament on March 24 was, in consequence, held with greater magnificence than usual. In this Shakespeare and Burbage played an unaccustomed part. It was the custom for the knights who took part in the tournament to carry paper shields known as *impresa* on which was painted a device and a motto which was supposed to reveal the bearer's state of mind. The *impresa* were collected and hung in a room in Whitehall, where they provided a pleasant guessing-game. Francis Manners, the Catholic Earl of Rutland, employed,

* The titles given in the Chamber Account are *Sir John Falstaff* and *Caesar's Tragedy*.

at the cost of £4 8s., William Shakespeare and Richard
Burbage (who had a reputation as a painter as well as an
actor) to design his shield for him. Such a combination of
talents should have been indeed impressive – Shakespeare
presumably invented the motto – but unfortunately it was
not. The only spectator who has left a record of the event
says that none of the emblems was a success except the
two carried by Pembroke and his brother, and that some
of the rest were so confused 'that their meaning is not yet
understood.'

The final festivity of the marriage was given in Kerr's
castle of Rochester (he had been created Viscount Rochester
in 1611), whither the King accompanied his daughter
and her husband on the way to Dover. On St George's
Day, Kerr was made a Knight of the Garter and a
week or two later, serious preparations were begun for his
marriage by the appointment of an official Ecclesiastical
Commission to enquire into the possible nullity of the existing marriage between the Earl of Essex and his Countess,
Frances Howard.

That summer, while the Commission was sitting, there was
a sinister undercurrent in London. For one thing, the
twenty-one-year-old Earl of Essex (the son of Elizabeth I's
Essex) objected to being publicly branded as impotent and
was not prepared to be as complaisant as was expected of
him. For another, Frances Howard was not altogether
certain of Kerr's infatuation. In consequence, she resorted
to witchcraft and spells to ensure beyond doubt his devotion
to her, as well as her husband's impotence. She visited, that is
to say, that ambiguous character, Simon Forman.

Forman, who was sixty-one at this time, had as a child
been troubled with hallucinations and visions. At fourteen
he had been apprenticed to an apothecary where he gained
a considerable knowledge of drugs. Having scraped togethei
enough money he had gone to Oxford as a 'poor scholar'
but had left without taking his degree. His main subject

of study seems to have been astrology and on leaving Magdalen he had set up for himself as an apothecary and fortune-teller. In 1588 he went further in his studies in the Black Art and started to practice necromancy, calling up spirits within the Magic Circle. By 1595, he was sufficiently proficient to be visited by Queen Elizabeth I's physician and four years later he went to Holland to learn the final mysteries of his profession from a circle of necromancers there. On his return to London, he became so notorious that he was summoned by the Society of Physicians for practising medicine without a degree and, to remedy the deficiency, went to Cambridge where, just after King James's accession, he obtained, at the age of fifty, a Doctorate of Physic and Astronomy. For the last ten years – from 1603 to 1613 – he had been, at his house in Lambeth, a power in London.

It is quite possible that Shakespeare knew him and in *Romeo and Juliet*, written just before the Queen's physician's visit, left a picture of him as he appeared on the verge of his success:

> I do remember an apothecary,
> And whereabouts 'a dwells, which late I noted
> In tatter'd weeds, with overwhelming brows
> Culling of simples; meagre were his looks,
> Sharp misery had worn him to the bones;
> And in his needy shop a tortoise hung,
> An alligator stuff'd and other skins
> Of ill-shaped fishes; and about his shelves
> A beggarly account of empty boxes,
> Green, earthen pots, bladders and musty seeds,
> Remnants of pack-thread, and old cakes of roses
> Were thinly scattered to make a show.

Whether or not Shakespeare knew him, there is no doubt that posterity is indebted to Forman for a knowledge of Shakespeare's work. For the necromancer was an inveterate

playgoer and his *Book of Plays* contains careful accounts of
the 1611 performances at the Globe of *Macbeth*, *Cymbeline*, and
The Winter's Tale.

At *Macbeth* he looked with a professional eye, on the one
hand describing the witches carefully as 'three women
fairies or Nymphs' and, on the other, noting: 'Observe how
Macbeth's Queen did rise in the night in her sleep and
walk and talked and confessed all, and the Doctor noted her
words.' He was apt to draw personal lessons from the plays
he saw and at the end of a *Richard II* (not Shakespeare's)
he wrote: 'Remember how the Duke of Lancaster asked a
Wise Man whether himself should ever be a king, and he
told him, No, but his son should be a king. And when he had
told him, he hanged him up for his labour, because he should
not bruit it abroad or speak thereof to others. This was policy
in the commonwealth's opinion; but I say it was a villain's
part and a Judas kiss to hang the man for telling the truth.
Beware by this example of noblemen and of their fair words
and say little to them, lest they do the like by thee for thy
good will.'

Though, as far as he could, he followed his own counsel
and acted with what discretion was possible, Forman trusted
Frances Howard when she came to consult him secretly.
He gave her powders, one of which was a love philtre for
Kerr, while the other, if put in her husband's food, would
have the effect of making him feel no attraction for her so
that she might indeed reproach him for impotence. He
modelled pictures and figures representing the three,
including a wax effigy of Frances 'sitting in form of a naked
woman, spreading and laying forth her hair in a looking-
glass' and 'a man and woman in copulation, made in lead'
and 'a figure in which was written the word Corpus and
upon the parchment was fastened a little piece of the skin
of a man,' as well as 'a parchment wherein were contained
all the names of the Blessed Trinity mentioned in the
Scriptures, and in another parchment +B+C+D+E.'

F

While these metaphysical aids, combined with the theological arguments of the Anglican Bishops on the Commission, were invoked on the side of the nullity suit, it was opposed with reckless bitterness and from comprehensible human motives by Sir Thomas Overbury, Kerr's intimate friend, who had been accurately described at Court as 'the Keeper of the King's Keeper.' They had first met in Scotland when Overbury was twenty and Kerr fourteen and the rising young diplomat, with a reputation as a poet which even Ben Jonson allowed, had immediately captivated the Earl of Dunbar's careless young page. 'So they came along to England together and were great friends.'* When Kerr was taken into the royal favour, Overbury remained at his side, acting as his mentor and secretary and guiding him in the unfamiliar ways of court. They remained, as they had been dubbed in Scotland, David and Jonothan. In the first instance, Overbury had approved Kerr's approach to Frances Howard, under the impression that it was a convenient flirtation which would increase his political influence. He had even written Kerr's love-letters for him. But as soon as he realised the truth, he turned bitterly against it. At one o'clock one morning, in the gallery at Whitehall, Kerr found Overbury waiting for him.

'How now,' said Kerr, 'are you up yet?'

'Nay,' retorted Overbury, 'what do you here at this time of night? Will you never leave the company of that base woman?'

They started to quarrel and Overbury flung at him: 'Well, my lord, if you do marry that filthy, base woman you will utterly ruin your honour and yourself; you shall never do it by my advice or consent; and, if you do, you had best look to stand fast.'

Kerr retorted: 'My own legs are straight and strong enough to bear me up, but, i' faith, I will be even with you for this.'

* 'A Book Touching Sir Thomas Overbury, with Notes taken A.D. 1637 from the mouth of Sir Nicholas Overbury, the father of Sir Thomas.'

'And so parted from him in a great rage.'

The scandal was now an open one. Kerr appealed to the
King, who was, in any case, jealous of Overbury. James
dealt with it in his own fashion. He offered Overbury a
diplomatic post in either Holland, France or Russia, which-
ever he preferred, and when Overbury refused sent him to
the Tower where he died in the agonies of slow poison
administered by the servants of Frances Howard, who had
obtained it from Simon Forman.

Ten days later – on September 25, 1613 – the Commission
reported that the Essex marriage was null, a verdict which
was 'discussed with a remarkable unanimity of abhorrence
in every corner of the land.' On December 26, Kerr (now
created Earl of Somerset so that his rank should not be
inferior to his bride's) married Frances Howard.

Thus the year 1614 opened with the triumph of the pro-
Spanish Howards and the unquestioned ascendancy of
Somerset. It seemed that nothing could touch the Favourite
except his own overbearing temperament, which was shortly
to provoke James to a memorable letter, in the course of
which he reminded the young man: 'You have, in many of
your mad fits, done what you can to persuade me that you
mean to hold me not so much by love as by awe, and that
you have me so far in my reverence as that I dare not offend
you or resist your appetites. I leave out of this reckoning
your long creeping back and withdrawing yourself from
lying in my chamber, notwithstanding my many hundred
times earnestly soliciting you to the contrary, accounting
that but as a point of unkindness . . . What shall be the
best remedy for this, I will tell you: Be kind. But for the
easing of my inward and consuming grief, all I crave is that
in all the words and actions of your life you may ever make
it appear to me that you never think to hold grip of me but
out of my mere love and not one hair by force. I told you
twice or thrice you might lead me by the heart and not by
the nose. If I ever find that you think to retain me by one

sparkle of fear, all the violence of my love will in that instant be changed into as violent a hatred.'

For seven years the two had been publicly inseparable. James was now forty-seven, Somerset twenty-seven. It was a danger-point in their emotional relationship, quite apart from the surrounding stresses. Somerset's danger was increased by the fact that he had no longer the perspicacious Overbury to guide him and that the anti-Spanish party, led by the Archbishop of Canterbury, Pembroke and his brother, and Sir Ralph Winwood who had just been made Secretary of State for life, were waiting their opportunity to overthrow him.

Their chance came on the 3rd of August that year when the King, on the summer Progress, visited Apthorpe in Northamptonshire and there set eyes on young George Villiers, an impecunious youth of twenty-one, whose effeminate beauty, with his soft expressive eyes, his full mouth, his 'very lovely complexion,' his long delicate hands, 'his limbs so well compacted' caused a Bishop to remark that 'from the nails of his fingers – nay, from the sole of his foot to the crown of his head, there was no blemish in him.'

Thus a new factor was introduced into English politics. The Royal interest in the young man was so obvious to onlookers that the Pembroke party realised that here was an instrument by which they might overturn the Howards and that in Villiers was a potential English and anti-Catholic candidate for the bedchamber who might displace the Scottish Somerset and turn the King's policy back to traditional channels.

The difficulties, even supposing Villiers were pliant and James's interest more than temporary, were considerable. It was only a fortnight since Somerset had been made Lord Chamberlain, which meant that any appointment would have to be made through him and as he, better than anyone in the kingdom, knew every move of the game, it would be impossible to elude his vigilance. There was, in addition,

the Queen to be won over, since James had made it a rule
that his favourite must be officially recommended by his
wife so that any subsequent recrimination on her part could
be silenced by a simple retort. And the Queen, with her
Catholic sympathies, was, though she detested Somerset,
unlikely to favour a nominee of the anti-Catholic faction.

Initially, however, things were allowed to take their
natural course, because Somerset was unexpectedly complaisant and, sure of his dominance of James, was not unwilling,
especially in view of his marriage, to be relieved of the burden
of undivided attention. Also, as he told the King, it was
politic occasionally to extend the Royal favour to young
Englishmen,* since thus the lie would be given to those who
complained that the Scots had a monopoly of it. The office
of cupbearer was bought for Villiers, though when an
attempt was made to get him a vacant post in the Bedchamber, Somerset considered that things had gone far
enough and insisted on it being given to his own nephew.

Villiers was powerless to further his fortune. The utmost
he could do was to exert his charm on all with whom he
came into contact and hope that his modest affability would
be compared favourably with Somerset's tempestuous arrogance. It might be true, as the Court gossips wrote, that
'in his passion of love to his new favourite, the King was more
impatient than any woman to enjoy her love' but outwardly
James remained loyal to the older affection. He asked
Somerset: 'What can or ever could trouble your mind?
Do not all courtesies and places come through your office
as Chamberlain? And have you not, besides, your infinite
privacy with me?' At the beginning of April, 1615, eight
months after the meeting at Apthorpe, the 'pretty, harmless,
affable gentleman' was still only a cupbearer, in spite of the
King's contribution of £1,500 to a new Twelfth Night

* James's last English favourite had been Pembroke's younger
brother, the Earl of Montgomery, who had sacrificed the position by
publicly spitting after James had publicly kissed him.

masque written by Ben Jonson, *Mercury vindicated from the Alchemists*, whose object was 'for the gracing of young Villiers and to bring him on the stage.' As one of the 'Sons of Nature' led in by Prometheus, he exhibited his dancing, an exercise in which he excelled, both by reason of 'the daintiness of his leg and foot' and because he 'had kept much company with the gentlemen waiters who sometimes after supper did leap and exercise their bodies.' Yet Villiers might have remained nothing more than a minor ornament of the Court and an admired dancer had not urgent political considerations forced Pembroke to act. Somerset had suggested that he himself should be allowed to treat secretly with Spain and thus circumvent the young Ambassador, Digby, who was keeping Pembroke and his party abreast with Spanish diplomatic secrets.

At a meeting of the party at Montgomery's town house in the neighbourhood of Blackfriars, it was determined to persuade the Queen to recommend Villiers for advancement to the Bedchamber. This, at the entreaty of the Archbishop of Canterbury, the Queen reluctantly agreed to do, though she warned them shrewdly enough: 'My lord, you and the rest of your friends know not what you do. I know your master better than you all: for if this young man be once brought in, the first persons that he will plague must be you that labour for him.' In after years, the Archbishop was to exclaim: 'Noble Queen, how like a prophetess you spake!' but at the time he advanced the argument that, as far as could be judged, Villiers had a pleasant nature and that, even if he had not, 'it would be a long time before he were able to attain to that height of evil which the other hath.'

While the Archbishop was persuading the Queen, the Baynard's Castle meeting was having other repercussions. As the Earls, with their retainers, were returning from London to Westminster along the highway of the Strand, one of the servants had thrown some mud at a portrait of

Somerset exposed for sale in a shop. The incident was duly
reported and, in return, one of Somerset's servants spilt a
bowl of soup over Villiers as he was waiting on the King at
table. Villiers in fury hit the man, whereupon Somerset
pointed out that the penalty for striking a blow in the Royal
Presence was the loss of the offender's right hand. He added
that, as Lord Chamberlain, it would be his pleasant duty
'to be ready at the time and place of execution to sear the
stump when the hand is stricken off.' This was the first
open trial of strength between the rivals and when James
pardoned Villiers on the ground that his action, though
technically illegal, was justified by the circumstances, the
courtiers decided that the younger man had gained 'a clear
conquest.'

On April 23, 1615, a few days later, he gained another.
That evening he stood chatting with Pembroke, Montgomery and the Archbishop of Canterbury outside the door
of the Royal Bedchamber. Across the room, Somerset,
surrounded by the Howards, scowled at him. Both parties,
as well as the lesser courtiers (who were now in a serious
quandary as to which man it was safer to flatter) knew what
was afoot. Behind the closed doors the Queen was urging
the King to make Villiers a Gentleman of the Bedchamber.
Somerset, acting for the moment in his capacity of Lord
Chamberlain, sent a message to the King recommending
him to bestow only the inferior office of Groom of the
Bedchamber. The Archbishop, overhearing it, sent a
message to the Queen entreating her to insist on the higher
post.

When eventually the Royal mind was officially made up,
the public proceedings were given an air of ingenuous
impromptu. The Queen, indicating Villiers, remarked that
here, on the Feast of England's patron saint, was a young
man named, appropriately enough, George, who was a
'candidate for the honour of knighthood, worthy of St
George himself.' The King agreed. The Queen asked Prince

Charles to bring her his father's sword. Charles, a sullen
boy of fourteen, obeyed. James, in spite of the rehearsal,
quailed when he saw his wife advancing on him with a drawn
sword. His terror of steel was, on any occasion, too involun-
tary to be controlled; on this occasion he was, additionally,
in a highly emotional state (not unconnected, the Archbishop thought, with being 'too powerfully refreshed at the
Festival of St George') and when he gave the accolade to
the kneeling Villiers, his hand had to be guided by the
Queen to prevent him poking his eye out. The ceremony
was, however, concluded without mishap and the new
Favourite arose Sir George Villiers with, to sustain the new
dignity, the post of Gentleman of the Bedchamber and
an income of £1,000 a year from the Court of Wards.
James, noticing a resemblance between his face and a
painting of St Stephen 'looking steadfastly up to Heaven,'
privately named him 'Steenie' and took him into the
Bedchamber.

The Progress that summer – the hot, dry summer of 1615
which produced such excellent grapes and melons – was
attended by both Somerset and Villiers and was, naturally, 'nothing but one faction braving the other.' The
final blow to Somerset's prestige was the King's decision
to celebrate the first anniversary of his meeting with Villiers
by breaking the planned itinerary and visiting Villiers's
mother. From that moment it was open war. Somerset threw
discretion to the winds, insulting Villiers and storming at the
King. He would be satisfied with nothing less than the dismissal of his rival. James retorted by telling him that,
although he was no longer sole favourite, he could still
retain most of his power if he patronised Villiers and
allowed him 'to take his rise under the show of his wings.'
But when Villiers came to him and, as he had been instructed
by the King, said: 'My Lord, I desire to be your servant
and your creature, and shall desire to take my Court
preferment under your favour.' Somerset returned the quick

answer: 'I will none of your service and you shall none of
my favour. I will, if I can, break your neck, and of that be
confident.' And 'since that time breaking each other's necks
was their aims.'

Villiers's twenty-third birthday was spent at Farnham
where he finally consolidated his position, if we are to trust
one of his letters in which he coyly reminded the King of
'that time I shall never forget at Farnham when the bed's
head could not be found between the master and his dog.'*
And a month later, when they were Southampton's guests
at Beaulieu, the final doom of Somerset was sealed.

An apothecary's boy had made a death-bed confession
that two years earlier had been employed by certain 'great
people' to put poison in Overbury's food in the Tower. The
matter, after its ramifications had been examined and its
truth established, was brought to the King's notice by Sir
Ralph Winwood, who rode down to Beaulieu to deliver the
information. James decided that the prosecution, whoever
might be implicated, must proceed. The net, spread wider,
enmeshed Somerset and his wife. The Lord Chief Justice,
who was presiding over the enquiry, demanded Somerset's
presence. The Earl refused to appear. James insisted that
he went and, at Royston, took farewell of him. An eyewitness
has recorded the parting: 'The Earl of Somerset never
parted from him with more seeming affection . . . The King
hung about his neck, slobbering his cheeks, saying: "For
God's sake, when shall I see thee again? On my soul, I shall
neither eat nor sleep until you come again." The Earl told
him "On Monday" (this being on the Friday). "For God's
sake let me," said the King, "Shall I? Shall I?" Then lolled
about his neck. Then: "For God's sake, give thy lady this
kiss from me." In the same manner at the stairs' head,
at the middle of the stairs, and at the stairs' foot. The Earl
was not in his coach when he used these very words: "I
shall never see his face more." '

* Villiers always signed himself 'Your Majesty's dog and slave.'

Nor did he. When Somerset wrote from London urging him at the eleventh hour to stop the case, James replied: 'If I should suffer a murder (if it be so) to be suppressed and plastered over, to the destruction of both my soul and reputation, I am no Christian. I never mean wittingly and willingly to bear any man's sins but my own.' The King's one desire was that Somerset should plead guilty, but this the Earl, who was undoubtedly innocent even of knowledge of his wife's murder of Overbury, refused to do, even with the assurance of a pardon. As the affair proceeded, the lesser culprits were tried and executed, though Forman himself was dead, and the time came when Somerset awaiting trial was transferred from house-arrest to the Tower.

Legend has synchronised his entry into Raleigh's room there with Raleigh's departure from it and made Raleigh say, as they passed each other, that 'his whole *History* had not the like precedent, of a King's chief prisoner to purchase freedom and his bosom favourite to have the halter, but in Scripture, Mordecai and Haman.' It is possible that they did in fact meet when Raleigh went back to collect the last of his belongings from prison, for the King is said to have glowered when he heard of the remark. It was one thing for love of Villiers to let Somerset suffer; it was quite another to justify the hated Raleigh. He sent back to Raleigh the menacing message 'that he might die in this deceit' – 'which he did,' the chronicler records, 'and Somerset saved.' Indeed some have seen James's eventual pardon of Somerset (who was, with his wife, in due course found guilty of murder), in part influenced by a determination to give Raleigh at this last the lie.

For the final six months of Shakespeare's life, this scandal in high places was the one paramount subject of gossip all over England. The last attempt of the King to persuade Somerset to plead 'Guilty' was made on the day that, in Stratford, Shakespeare gave away his daughter Judith in

marriage to Richard Quiney. The entry of Somerset into
the Tower in March coincided with the time when, in his
illness, Shakespeare made his will. If, in the April, Ben
Jonson actually visited him for the legendary drinking-bout,
the trial about to begin and the persons concerned must
have been one of the subjects of conversation, especially
since Ben had written his best masque, appropriately
entitled *The Golden Age Restored*, set in the Palace of Cupid,
for a Twelfth Night celebration of Somerset's fall and
Villiers's triumph.

In life, Villiers's triumph was reserved for the day Shakespeare died, when he was made Knight of the Garter, on his
recovery from the attack of smallpox which might have
ended his looks and his favour. He was the Junior Knight-
Elect. The Senior Knight-Elect (who was later to be his
father-in-law) was that Earl of Rutland for whom Shakespeare
and Burbage, three years earlier, had designed their un-
noticed shield.

For Villiers the only cloud on the proceedings was the
news that Somerset, in the Tower, was ostentatiously
wearing his Garter.

For Shakespeare, it might have been relevant to know
that his own 'lovely boy,' Southampton, now a grizzled
man of forty-three, was also, of right, at that St George's
Feast, with his dynasty safe and his son and heir nine,
having answered his friend's plea, made a lifetime ago:

When forty winters shall besiege thy brow
And dig deep trenches in they beauty's field,
Thy youth's proud livery, so gaz'd on now,
Will be a tattered weed, of small worth held;
Then, being asked were all thy beauty lies,
Where all the treasure of thy lusty days,
To say, within thine own deep-sunken eyes,
Were an all-eating shame and thriftless praise.
How much more praise deserved thy beauty's use,

If thou coulds't answer 'This fair child of mine
Shall sum my count and make my old excuse,'
Proving his beauty by succession thine!

It was Shakespeare who died without a son. Nor was there to be any male heir of his short line to inherit the perishable things he had so carefully garnered.

XVII : Noll

WHEN James of Scotland, in the spring of 1603, came
slowly south to London, he was entertained with a
magnificence which left a lasting impression on his mind by
Sir Oliver Cromwell, High Sheriff and Member of Parliament for the county of Huntingdon, at his house at Hinchinbrook.

The Cromwells, descended from the favourite nephew of
Thomas Cromwell, Henry VIII's destroyer of the monasteries, had inherited considerable spoils in East Anglia.
Sawtry Abbey, St Neot's Priory, Hinchinbrook Nunnery, a
large part of the holdings of Ramsey Abbey and the house
of St Mary of the Austin Canons in Huntingdon itself were
but part of their acquisition. Sir Henry Cromwell, Sir
Oliver's father, had built on the site of and partly out of the
actual buildings of Hinchinbrook Nunnery, a magnificent
mansion, which his eldest son, Sir Oliver, when he inherited
it, continued to improve. Sir Henry's second son, Robert,
who lived as quietly as his elder brother lived ostentatiously,
was given the property in Huntingdon, a mile from Hinchinbrook, where he lived in a house which had once been part
of the Hospital of St John and drew his income from the farms
and tithes which had once belonged to the Austin Canons.

King James, travelling from the North, reached Huntingdon on April 27, 1603. There he was met by the Earl of
Southampton, not long released from his imprisonment
in the Tower, and come to thank His Majesty for his enlargement. The Bailiff of Huntingdon gave James the Sword of

State, which the King gave to Southampton to bear before him on the remainder of the journey to Hinchinbrook.

Sir Oliver received the Royal party at the gate of the Great Court and conducted him to the principal entrance to the house, where, for two days, James was given such hospitality as he had never before known. Indeed, it was said at the time that 'it was the greatest feast that had been given to a king by a subject.' Moreover, Sir Oliver threw the house open to all who wished to share in it, as an expression of loyalty, and 'each individual was welcomed with the choicest viands and most costly wines: even the populace had free access to the cellars, during the whole of His Majesty's stay.' From Cambridge, the heads of the university came in their robes to congratulate James on his accession in a long Latin oration.

The King remained at Hinchinbrook until April 29, when his host presented him, as a leaving-present, with 'a large and elegant wrought cup of gold, goodly horses, deep-mouthed hounds, divers hawks of excellent wing, and gave fifty pounds among the royal officers.' James showed his appreciation by creating Sir Oliver a Knight of the Bath and by returning to Hinchinbrook no less than four times during the first three years of his reign to occupy the State Bed which was kept for him in the Velvet Room.

At this first visit, Robert Cromwell's son, Oliver (who had been named after his uncle), was four. Thus, by the time he was seven, Noll was accustomed enough to the Stuart family with whom, on his mother's side, he was distantly connected. One story, which, in spite of its symbolic appropriateness, may be true is that, on one of these occasions when the King had Prince Charles (who was a year younger than Oliver) with him 'Sir Oliver sent for his nephew Oliver that he might play with his Royal Highness; but they had not been long together before Charles and Oliver disagreed; and as the former was then as weakly as the latter was strong, it was no wonder that the royal visitant was worsted; and

Oliver, even at this age, so little regarded dignity that he made the royal blood flow in copious streams from the Prince's nose. This was looked on as a bad presage for that king when the civil wars commenced.'

The King was again at Hinchinbrook in the winter of 1610, with Robert Kerr at his side, and on that occasion wrote from there his angry letter to the Privy Council, complaining of the conduct of the Commons, who were showing reluctance to allow him to indulge himself and Kerr with the riches of his English subjects, to the existence of which the splendour of Sir Oliver Cromwell's hospitality had first opened his eyes. 'Our fame and actions have been tossed like tennis-balls among them,' he complained, 'and all that spite and malice durst do to disgrace and inflame us hath been used. To be short, this Lower House by their behaviour have perilled and annoyed our health, wounded our reputation, emboldened an ill-natured people, encroached upon many of our privileges and plagued our purse with their delays.'

There can be little doubt that Kerr himself was behind this attitude of James's. The Commons had bitterly criticised the King's favourite. One Member had pointedly remarked that it was 'unfit and dishonourable that those should waste the treasure of the State who take no pains to live of their own but expend all in excess and riot, depending wholly upon the bounty of the Prince.' There was a rumour, which reached the King, that shortly Members intended before they granted any money to petition him to send all Scots back to their own country. Upon this, Kerr became seriously alarmed and did all that he could to inflame the King against the Commons; and in James's letter to the Speaker, ordering him to adjourn the House, the King wrote that he could not have 'asinine patience' and that he would refuse to accept the largest grant Parliament could give him if they 'were to sauce it with such taunts and disgraces as' had 'been uttered of him and those that appertained to him.' One can almost hear Kerr's voice reproaching his master for having 'the patience of an ass.'

Oliver Cromwell, eleven at the time of this episode, was being educated, with the other boys of Huntingdon, by Dr Thomas Beard, who was also the Rector of St John's – which church the Robert Cromwells attended – an author, a figure in local affairs and a friend of the family. At school Oliver was undergoing the usual Grammar School training prescribed for those between the ages of five and fifteen (a curriculum not differing greatly from that at Stratford when Shakespeare was at school thirty-five years earlier) – English, Latin, arithmetic, geometry, logic, rhetoric and a little Greek. But it was not at these that Noll excelled, but at 'throwing the stone or bar, tennis, wrestling, running, swimming, handling weapons, riding, hunting, dancing and shooting with the long bow.' Whatever he may have thought of the King and the weakly Prince Charles and the Favourite, 'Noll,' who was to become the greatest cavalry leader in the world, would certainly have approved Henry, Prince of Wales's exploit in making an epic ride to Hinchinbrook through the heat of an August night.

This Royal visit to the Cromwells was made in 1612 at the height of Henry's quarrel with Kerr and James. The Prince had refused to go on the autumn Progress with his father. James had peremptorily ordered it and insisted that Henry should join him at Belvoir Castle in Nottinghamshire. Henry, furious, left obedience to the last moment. 'His Highness neither considering the strength of his body, the greatness of the journey (being near four-score and sixteen miles) nor the extreme and wonderful heat of the season, determined to ride that great journey in two days; according to which he set forth on Friday by one of the clock in the morning from his house at Richmond, coming to Hinchinbrook by ten of the clock in the morning, which, as they say, is three-score miles in nine hours posting, where he remained all night, the next day having six-and-thirty miles to Belvoir

Castle, where he met his father just at the time prefixed.'

For the next four years there were no incursions of royalty at Hinchinbrook, but the stories of the Essex nullity suit, the Somerset-Howard marriage and the scandal of Over-bury's murder must have made their impact on Hinchinbrook and Huntingdon as on every other corner of the kingdom and the various revelations of the condition of the Court can have had only the effect of confirming the Puritanism of the Robert Cromwells and Dr Beard, the home and school atmosphere which the growing Oliver absorbed.

It was the character of Beard especially which moulded the boy. He was a Puritan whose book *The Theatre of God's Judgments* (which went into four editions, the second being published when Oliver was twelve) was concerned to stress God's immediate presence and His interest in every petty detail of men's lives. It was full of examples of angelic or Satanic intervention in daily life; of retribution for the wicked and salvation for the good – especially when the good were also poor. It was shot through with hatred for Rome, which was equated with anti-Christ, and with the certainty of triumph for the Elect who obeyed God's laws 'and consequently the laws of man and nature.' Religion was not a matter of forms and ceremonies or even of speculation and philosophy, but an exciting and tempestuous melo-drama being continuously performed from day to day, the God and the Devil heading the cast.

Beard not only saw life and religion in terms of the theatre, but he wrote short classical comedies with unimpeachable endings for his pupils to perform. Occasionally they acted plays by other authors, and it is a paradox indeed that Cromwell at Huntingdon got more practice in acting than Shakespeare at Stratford.

One of these plays in which Noll is known to have made an appearance was Anthony Brewer's *Lingua, or the Combat of the Tongue and the Five Senses*. The play had been printed and first acted at Trinity College, Cambridge, in 1607 – a year

in which, because of one of the periodical outbreaks of the
plague, Shakespeare's company was touring from July to
December and probably visited Cambridge with *All's Well
that Ends Well*, in which Shakespeare himself was playing
the Duke. There could hardly have been a greater difference
between that and Brewer's academic effort in derivative
blank-verse, which tells how Lingua gives a crown and a robe
to be contended for by the senses. Oliver was Tactus, the
sense of Touch. In one scene, with Mendacio, the liar, he is
gazing upward and trips over the robe and crown:

> *Tactus:* High thoughts have slippery feet. I had well nigh
> fallen.
> *Mendacio:* Well doth he fall who riseth with a fall.
> *Tactus:* What's this?
> *Mendacio:* O, are you taken? It is vain to strive.

Nevertheless Tactus takes the crown and robe and indulges
in a soliloquy:

> Was ever man so fortunate as I
> To break his shins at such a stumbling-block?
> Roses and bays back hence! This crown and robe
> My brows and body circles and invests:
> How gallantly it fits me! Sure the slave
> Measured my head that wrought this coronet.
> They lie who say complexions cannot change,
> My blood's ennobled and I am transformed
> Unto the sacred temper of a King.
> Methinks I hear my noble parasites
> Styling me Caesar or great Alexander,
> Licking my feet, and wondering where I got
> This precious ointment, how my pace is mended,
> How princely do I speak, how sharp I threaten.
> Peasants, I'll curb your headstrong impudence
> And made you tremble when the lion roars;
> Ye earth-bred worms! O for a looking-glass!
> Poets will write whole volumes on this change.

Whole volumes indeed have been written on Oliver and few
have omitted this incident, which, according to one of his
first biographers, 'particularly affected him.' Its prophetic
appropriateness is, indeed, clear enough, but its implications are both deeper and less obvious; for it was to the
dramatic sense in Dr Beard that the true temperament of
Oliver responded most surely.

The ethics and thought-forms, the eccelesiastical and
political postulates of Beard's teaching were for him reinforced from many sides – negatively by the character of the
Court, positively by the Puritan training of his home. The
personal apprehension of sin and salvation which, later,
he was to undergo was, of necessity, a unique individual
experience. As a child of his age, at once circumscribed and
compelled by his circumstances, he expressed himself in the
belief and action available to him. But the dynamic force,
which underlay and conditioned all, was timeless and found
its counterpart in the instinct which leads all great men –
Alexander no less than a St Augustine – to their destiny,
the instinct, indefinable but unmistakable, which is that
sixth sense called a 'sense of theatre.'

Puritan mystic, cavalry commander, King breaker, subtle
politician, ruler, Oliver's eventual diversity was unified by
this constant apprehension of the world in terms of the
theatre. To him, as to all dynamic characters, every action,
natural and supernatural, was dramatic action. His enemies
who called him an actor were, though they meant it as a
synonym for hypocrite, defining more exactly than they
knew. No man on the stage of history ever had a surer
instinct for exits and entrances, for the balance of speech
and silence, for the interplay of suspense and decision,
for the uses of surprise and the understanding of dramatic
irony. Because he was, in a profound sense, an actor, he
was able to play his part in the Theatre of God's Judgments.

It is of some significance that, in spite of many attempts, no
one has been able to write a satisfactory play about him. The

only man who might have done it died two days before
Oliver's sixteenth birthday.

On that day, April 23, 1616, Oliver entered Sidney
Sussex, the new Puritan college at Cambridge. The choice
was significant, for Sidney Sussex was to be the stronghold
of the extremists, political and religious, and Oliver's father,
Robert, had been at Queen's, to which it might have been
expected that he would send his son. The Master of Sidney
was Samuel Ward, who had been one of the translators
of the 1611 version of the Bible and was later to attend the
Calvinistic Synod of Dort. He impressed his somewhat timid
personality on his little domain. The chapel had no statues
and no stained glass. The Prayer Book was followed only
sufficiently to comply with the law. Cromwell's tutor, Howlet,
was a man of little consequence and, indeed, few if any of
the tutors were of any distinction. The students were of a
similar calibre. Oliver was one of less than a dozen gentlemen-
commoners.

Not that, in Oliver's case, it mattered greatly. His aversion
to study continued. His tutor is said to have noticed that
'neither was he then so much addicted to Speculation as to
Action' and a later biographer put it more brutally when he
wrote: 'During his short residence there . . . he was more
famous for his exercise in the Fields than in the Schools
(in which he never had the honour of, because no worth and
merit to, a degree) being one of the chief match-makers and
players at Foot-ball, Cudgels or any other boysterous sport
or game.' He stayed at Cambridge only a year, when, on
his father's death, he returned to Huntingdon to take up the
burdens of manhood.

The cardinal burden of the Civil War and its consequences
was more than a quarter of a century in the future. It was not
until after Naseby when he was marching westward on
the final 'mopping-up' operations that Cromwell came to
Stratford and for two summer days quartered his troops
there. At New Place, Shakespeare's daughter, Susanna,

now sixty-two, still lived with her daughter Elizabeth, and her son-in-law, Thomas Nash. But Dr Hall had been dead for ten years and the Nashes had no children.

Cromwell's own choice of lodging would certainly not have been there, but with the Combes, who were Puritans and Parliamentarians, while the Nashes were among the few Royalists in the town. And at New Place, two years earlier, in the July of 1643, the Queen Henrietta Maria herself had stayed on her way to take her last farewell of King Charles, her husband. She was entertained there by Prince Rupert and what splendours of the Court were left came incongruously into Shakespeare's garden. It is doubtful whether Henrietta had any sense of honour done her, or whether, absorbed in her own preoccupations in playing at war (she called herself the 'She Generalissima'), she told Susanna that King Charles possessed a fine edition of the works of William Shakespeare, which he had carefully annotated with his own hand.

XVIII: Last Word

A<small>MONG</small> the tributary poems which prefaced the First
Folio were some lines by the young John Milton:

> We wonder'd, Shakespeare, that thou went'st so soon
> From the world's stage to the grave's tiring-room:
> We thought thee dead: but this thy printed worth
> Tells thy spectators that thou went'st but forth
> To enter with applause. An actor's art
> Can die, and live to act a second part:
> That's but an *exit* of mortality.
> This a re-entrance to a *plaudite*.

The re-entrance has been continuous: and in his prescience
of the power of the printed word, Milton was only echoing
Shakespeare's own certainty of their survival. Except that
Shakespeare was thinking of them in terms of the Sonnets,
not the plays: and of his love, not of himself. He had once
written to Southampton:

> Not marble, nor the gilded monuments
> Of princes, shall outlive this powerful rime:
> But you shall shine more bright in these contents
> Than unswept stone, besmear'd with sluttish time.
> When wasteful war shall statues overturn,
> And broils root out the work of masonry,
> Nor Mars his sword nor war's quick fire shall burn
> The living record of your memory.
> 'Gainst death and all-oblivious enmity

Shall you pace forth: your praise shall still find room
Even in the eyes of all posterity
That wears this world out to the ending doom.
    So, till the judgment that yourself arise,
    You live in this, and dwell in lovers' eyes.

So, in a final glance at the day Shakespeare died, it may be
a courtesy he would not despise to see it in terms of Southampton. Henry Wriothesley had, from the beginning, been
his link with the 'great' world. In his early years in London,
the young Earl had given private protection to his Faith
and public patronage to his genius. Through him, the actor
had become involved in politics and seen something of the
reality of the struggle for power. Through him, vicariously,
he had experienced the vicissitudes of eminence. In his friendship for him he had known the meaning of that love of which
the morals of James's Court were an obscene parody. And
now, at the end, Southampton still linked the three who
shared the events of St George's Day, 1616, with the dying
man.

At that very moment Southampton was, as a Knight of
the Garter, in Villiers's company at the Feast of St George at
Whitehall. To Raleigh, seeking help for new discoveries,
Southampton, with his life-long interest in the New World,
would be a sympathetic helper. With Oliver Cromwell
and his uncle at Hinchinbrook he would be the better
acquainted because, since his first meeting with the King
there, he had acquired a house in their neighbourhood,
where his heir had been born.

The Earl continued to play his part, as of right, in events
which were but life's untidy imitations of the dramas his
poet had created. Involved by his birth in ephemeral
greatness, it may be questioned whether Southampton
realised in what his own value consisted or would have
welcomed it if he had. Yet, that day, through the splendour
and pageantry at Whitehall, the careful etiquette and the

savage gossip, the ambitions and the fears and the seeds
of an unpredictable future, there may have stirred a memory
of immortal words he had once provoked:

No longer mourn for me when I am dead
Than you shall hear the surly sullen bell
Give warning of the world that I am fled
From this vile world, with vilest worms to dwell:
Nay, if you read this line, remember not
The hand that writ it; for I love you so,
That I in your sweet thoughts would be forgot
If thinking on me then should make you woe.

Index